Raymond Chandler

Twayne's United States Authors Series

Kenneth Eble, Editor

University of Utah

TUSAS 508

Raymond Chandler and Billy Wilder
Photograph courtesy of University Research Library, U.C.L.A.

Raymond Chandler

By William Marling

Case Western Reserve University

Twayne Publishers
A Division of G.K. Hall & Co. • Boston

Raymond Chandler

William Marling

Copyright © 1986 by G.K. Hall & Co.
All Rights Reserved
Published by Twayne Publishers
A Division of G.K. Hall & Co.
70 Lincoln Street
Boston, Massachusetts 02111

Copyediting supervised by Lewis DeSimone
Book production by Elizabeth Todesco
Book design by Barbara Anderson

Typeset in 11 pt. Garamond
by P&M Typesetting, Inc., Waterbury, Connecticut

Printed on permanent/durable acid-free paper
and bound in the United States of America

Library of Congress Cataloging in Publication Data

Marling, William, 1951–
   Raymond Chandler.

   (Twayne's United States authors series; TUSAS 508)
   Bibliography: p. 160
   Includes index.
   1. Chandler, Raymond, 1888–1959.   2. Detective and
mystery stories, American—History and criticism.
3. Authors, American—20th century—Biography.
I. Title.   II. Series.
PS3505.H3224Z73   1986   813'.52   86-7678
ISBN 0-8057-7472-6

For my parents,
Henry and Fern Marling

Contents

About the Author

William Marling received his B.A. from the University of Utah, and worked for *Fortune* and *Money* magazines, among other publications, before earning his Ph.D. from the University of California, Santa Barbara in 1980. His book *William Carlos Williams and the Painters* appeared in 1982. In 1983 he published *Dashiell Hammett* in this series and taught as a Fulbright Lecturer in Spain. He currently teaches at Case Western Reserve University in Cleveland.

Preface

The stories of Raymond Chandler have a way of turning detractors of the detective novel into devotees. The casual reader of *Farewell, My Lovely* comes away quoting its similes; literary critics read *The Long Goodbye* and realize that the mystery novel can, while fulfilling its obligations to a genre, be an instrument of self-insight and social criticism.

Small wonder that Chandler is generally considered to be the premier American mystery writer of the twentieth century. Exactly how his fictions work, however, has remained somewhat unclear. The writer himself was a paradox. After thirty years in the United States, he remained an Anglophile. A classicist by training, he was somewhat ashamed of making a living in "pulp" literature. An incurable romantic, he became famous as a "hard-boiled" realist.

There was clearly a great gap between the man and the genre. In this study I argue that the perspective afforded by this gulf allowed Chandler to push the limits of the genre further than anyone conceived they could stretch. An outsider, with a stake in America, he perceived the national myths clearly and put them to work with the appreciation of a classicist, and later pushed the conventions of their usage to the utmost limit. A poet in his youth, he introduced style into the genre and showed, as poets know, that metaphor is an expression of mythic impulse.

In writing this volume, I sought to frame a study that would be of continuing use to scholar and student. The seven novels have been in paperback since 1976; the major stories in similar editions since 1972. These volumes form my core texts, since they are the canon for all practical purposes. I have attempted to let the reader benefit as much as possible from the rich biography by Frank MacShane. As in the case of Dashiell Hammett, the events of Chandler's early life are enormously important to an understanding of his fiction.

The first three chapters cover Chandler's life and detail the history of the genre as well as the pulp magazine world in which Chandler started out. Publication data and immediate critical feedback on each book are included, to better portray the momentum of Chandler's career. The fourth chapter covers the short stories, including some that are not anthologized but thematically important. Chapter 5 examines *The Big Sleep* and *Farewell, My Lovely,* focusing on their plots and metaphoric sparkle. The sixth chapter concerns *The High Window* and *The Lady in the Lake,* novels Chandler wrote during World War II and his Hollywood period. His screenplays have been treated in several fine books and are not covered in this study. The seventh chapter examines the darker vision of *The Little Sister* and *The Long Goodbye,* undoubtedly Chandler's masterpiece. *Playback,* a lesser work, is included in chapter 8 with the summation.

A note of thanks must go to David Zeidberg and the Special Collections staff of the University Research Library at U.C.L.A., whose resources were invaluable. William F. Nolan supplied me with rare materials on and stimulating conversation about Chandler. Kurt Nutting sent me editions I never would have seen; Joe Golsan loaned me books and French criticism of Chandler that broadened my perspective immeasurably, as did the Spanish scholarship sent by Juan Villar Degano. My colleague P. K. Saha introduced me to the proper linguists.

In place of the usual accolade to my patient typist, I must offer tribute to the IBM personal computer and Wordstar, which formed this book from its outline to its footnotes.

William Marling

Case Western Reserve University

Acknowledgments

The Little Sister © 1949 by Raymond Chandler. © renewed 1976 by Helga Greene. Reprinted by permission of Houghton Mifflin Company. *The Long Goodbye* © 1953 by Raymond Chandler. © renewed 1981 by Helga Greene, executrix of the author. Reprinted by permission of Houghton Mifflin Company. *Playback* © 1958 by Raymond Chandler. Reprinted by permission of Houghton Mifflin Company. *The Simple Art of Murder* © 1950 by Raymond Chandler. © renewed 1978 by Helga Greene. Reprinted by permission of Houghton Mifflin Company. *Pickup on Noon Street* © 1950 by Raymond Chandler. © renewed 1978 by Helga Greene. Reprinted by permission of Houghton Mifflin Company. *Killer in the Rain* © 1950 by Raymond Chandler. © renewed 1978 by Helga Greene. Reprinted by permission of Houghton Mifflin Company. *Farewell, My Lovely* © 1940, *The High Window* © 1942, *The Lady in the Lake* © 1943, *The Big Sleep* © 1939, by Raymond Chandler. © renewed 1975 by Helga Greene. Reprinted by permission of Alfred A. Knopf, Inc. *The Life of Raymond Chandler* © 1976 by Frank MacShane. Reprinted by permission of E. P. Dutton. *Selected Letters of Raymond Chandler* © 1981 College Trustees Ltd. and Columbia University Press. Reprinted by permission of Helga Greene. Frontispiece reprinted by permission of University Research Library, U.C.L.A.

Chronology

1947   Writes screenplay of *Playback* for Universal.

1949   *The Little Sister.*

1950   *The Simple Art of Murder.*

1952   Vacations in London with his ailing wife.

1953   *The Long Goodbye.*

1954   Wife Cissy dies after long illness.

1955   Attempts suicide, moves to London.

1956–1957   Lives alternately in London and La Jolla.

1958   *Playback*

1959   Dies in La Jolla on 26 March.

Chapter One
Laramie to London

Raymond Chandler liked to say that he "was conceived in Laramie, Wyoming, and if they had asked me, I should have preferred to be born there." He explained that Chicago, where he was born 23 July 1888, "is not a place where an Anglophile would choose to be born."[1]

The remark is revealing. Chandler was indeed an Anglophile, a devotee of Henry James, a man of manners who sometimes looked askance at America and Americans. On the other hand, the American frontier—Chicago was little more in 1888—was Chandler's birthright. For a young man coming of age in England, his birthplace gave him a uniqueness and an excuse for his rebelliousness and inclination toward a career as a writer. Like Kipling's India, his birthplace was exotic and hindered his full assimilation. His Irish heredity compounded the problem. So he exaggerated his position beyond the social pale, staking his claim on the "frontier." And Laramie had a more romantic ring than Chicago did.

Chicago was the eastern terminus of a stretch of railroad maintained by the writer's father, Maurice Benjamin Chandler of Philadelphia, who worked as an engineer, probably for the Union Pacific. The writer's mother, Florence Dart Thornton, emigrated from Ireland to Plattsmouth, Nebraska, where she had relatives, around 1885. Maurice Chandler worked frequently in nearby Omaha, the midpoint of the Chicago-to-Laramie track. How the romance began is unclear, but the couple married at the western terminus of Chandler's section, then moved to the eastern end.

While Maurice was out repairing track, Florence Chandler and her son lived with relatives in Plattsmouth. Five decades later Chandler retained distinct memories of his midwestern childhood: "I remember the oak trees and the high wooden sidewalks beside the dirt roads and the heat and the fireflies and walking-sticks and a lot of strange insects and the gathering of wild grapes in the fall to make wine and the dead cattle and once in a while a dead man floating down the muddy river and the dandy little three-hole privy behind the house. I remember Ak-Sar-Ben and the days when they were still trying to

elect Bryan. I remember the rocking chairs on the edge of the sidewalk in a solid row outside the hotel and tobacco spit all over the
place."[2]

While quite young, Chandler had scarlet fever in a hotel room: "I
remember principally the ice cream and the pleasure of pulling the
loose skin off during convalescence" (*SL*, 235). He recalled that when
his father came home, he drank excessively. The Chandlers eventually
separated, then divorced. Chandler seldom spoke of his father and
then only to call him "an utter swine." Maurice Chandler disappeared, leaving his wife to raise their son, his son to invent a father.[3]

Yet it was not an unhappy beginning. As his biographer notes,
"Chandler's memories of the Middle West reveal a certain delight in
the modest and informal life of Plattsmouth. It was easy going and
relaxed, and at the same time a breeding ground for confidence trick-
sters. The Nebraska of Chandler's youth seems to have been a highly
suitable preparation for the Los Angeles he eventually was to describe."[4] Moreover, it was still *frontier,* with all such an environment
implies for personal and public morality. Later in life Chandler wrote
about the uncle with whom he and his mother spent time: "He used
to come home in the evening . . . put the paper on the music rack
and improvise [on the piano] while he read it. . . . He had a brother
who was an amazing character. He had been a bank clerk or manager
in a bank in Waterford, Ireland (where all my mother's people come
from, but none of them were Catholics) and had embezzled money.
He cleaned out the till one Saturday and, with the help of the Ma-
sons, escaped the police net to the continent of Europe. In some hotel
in Germany his money was stolen, or most of it. When I knew him,
long after, he was an extremely respectable old party, always immacu-
lately dressed, and of an incredible parsimony (*SL*, 41).

At age seven Chandler's life changed. His mother took him from
the high grass and loose morals of the plains to the coiffured parks
and gentility of London, to live with her sister and mother. Florence
Chandler's brother, a solicitor in Waterford, Ireland, had bought a
house for their mother to live in after their father's death. The grandmother and one "plain" sister who had not eloped to escape her tyranny ran the household as a matriarchy. Chandler's mother, the unfortunate beauty returned in disgrace, was made to feel her ignominy.

The women treated little Ray, the only male around, as the man
of the house, though he had little idea of what that role entailed. He
developed his own standard, which placed great value on women and

on loyalty to them, and he resented the treatment the grandmother and sister accorded his mother. The Irish, he learned, were somehow outside of English society. He gained a sense of justice, writes his biographer, "that became a central part of his character and gave him the attitudes he was to express later through his character Philip Marlowe."[5]

During the summer Chandler and his mother visited her brother, Ernest Thornton, in Waterford, Ireland. Thornton disliked the law, but practiced it to support his family's income and social pretensions, as well as his mother's London household. At a most impressionable age Chandler discovered class distinctions. The Thorntons were Protestant and looked down on Catholics, against whom they practiced all the subtle discriminations they learned in London. "What a strange sense of values we had," wrote Chandler. "What godawful snobs! My grandmother referred to one of the nicest families we knew as 'very respectable people' because there were two sons, five golden haired but unmarriagable daughters and no servant. They were driven to the utter humiliation of opening their own front door" (*SL*, 367).

But Chandler absorbed this value system. "When I was about seventeen," he recalled, "I was invited over to [a] house to play tennis. . . . A number of the guests were very young girls and young men, all expensively dressed, and several rather drunk. I was in no way expensively dressed, but far from feeling inferior I realized at once that these people were not at all up to the standard even of Dulwich, and heaven knows what Eton or Rugby would have thought about them. The boys and girls had gone to private schools, but not the right kind. There was a little something about their accents, and more than a little about their manners. (One sicked up in the drawing room.) During the course of an afternoon of rather studied courtesy on my part the family dog chewed up my straw hat with the school ribbon on it. When I left, the head of the family, a very nice little man in some kind of 'trade' in the City, insisted on paying for the hat. I coldly refused to accept his money, although in those times it was quite usual for the host to tip a schoolboy at the end of a visit. But this seemed to me different. This was taking money from a social inferior: not to be thought of" (*SL*, 368–69).

Chandler wanted to be English rather than Irish. "I am not an Irish-American in the sense commonly understood. I am of Quaker descent on both sides. The Irish family my mother belonged to had not a single Catholic relative or connection, even by marriage." He wrote this in 1940, trying to dissociate himself from the stereotype of the Irish working class. "Furthermore, the professional classes in Southern Ireland are and always have been largely non-Catholic. Those few Irish patriots who have had brains as well as spite have also been non-Catholics" (*SL*, 15–16).

But Ireland marked Chandler. It showed him hypocrisy and sham, and undoubtedly introduced him to the ancient Irish ways of disapproving of them: satire, irony, hyperbole, and wordplay. From the time of the *Tain* and legends of Cuchulain through the ages of Jonathan Swift and Flann O'Brien, Irish writers have said what they meant by saying something else. Ireland made him want to be English, yet reminded him that he was not. He had been born in a classless society, raised on a frontier, and transplanted into milieus in which birth and manners were all. Always a quick student, Chandler developed an eye for social detail, an appreciation of fine differences of speech and manner. His English education honed this ability and taught him that these differences were essential. Yet his American and Irish heritages never let him believe fully in such distinctions and later led him to ridicule such systems.

The Public School Background

In 1900 the Chandler household moved to Dulwich, where there was an excellent college preparatory school. The Dulwich School had begun to thrive under headmaster A. H. Gilkes, who introduced educational reforms such as courses in engineering and commerce and helped his boys win more than their share of scholarships to Oxford and Cambridge. Dulwich gave Chandler his intellectual lineaments, his ethics, his self-discipline—his whole outlook.

In his first session twelve-year-old Raymond took mathematics, music, Latin, French, divinity, and the history and geography of England. He played rugby, attended the classical music recitals for which the school was famous, and ended the year second among the twenty-eight boys in his form. But he was differentiating himself. He used his first name, like an American, instead of going by his initials, and carried a small notebook, in which he wrote down things that interested him.[6]

In his second year Chandler moved from university preparatory to commercial training classes. His family thought this more practical, given the necessity that he earn a living. Instead of the classics, he took French, Spanish, and German, focusing on correspondence and conversation. At the end of the year he ranked first in the form, winning prizes for mathematics and general achievement. In the third year Chandler changed back to the classical side. Dulwich College became famous that year, defeating well-known English and French soccer teams and winning an exceptional number of Oxford and Cambridge scholarships. But Chandler missed the excitement; he was often ill and had to make up work in Latin and Greek.

Through the fall of 1903 Chandler worked on his deficiencies. He was ranked first and advanced to the Upper Fifth in spring, where he continued math and German from the commercial program, and read his way through Caesar, Livy, Ovid, and some of the *Aeneid* in Latin, and Plato, Aristotle, Thucydides, and the Gospel of St. Mark in Greek. He worked on French, on Roman history, and studied Shakespeare, Addison, and Milton in English. In 1904 he changed courses again, this time to the Remove Form, for those boys not going to the universities. There Chandler was supposed to be "finished" under the hand of one of Dulwich's master teachers, but he fell ill. He left school in April 1905.

The Dulwich education, and the public school code, stayed with Chandler through his life. Headmaster Gilkes believed that education was the revelation of a moral order in life: literature was instruction, Greek and Roman history showed the role of ethics, the Bible illustrated the ideals of public service, altruism, and honor. Gilkes taught that egotism, brashness, and immodesty were the devils of modern life. Manliness meant forgetfulness of self, said Gilkes: a man of honor is one who is "capable of understanding that which was good; capable of subordinating the poorer part of his nature to the higher part."[7] This code is common to English public schools, but Gilkes was an unusually convincing advocate. He personified the code in his presence, and he made fine moral distinctions in everyday life.

Gilkes was also a writer, a published novelist who read his favorite passages aloud to his students. He queried them on their favorite parts, attempting to have them discover the effectiveness of prose rhythms, sentence structures, and diction. He also required essays, which he dissected, sentence by sentence, making them cut adjectives and break up long sentences. "Another common exercise in the mastery of language," notes Chandler's biographer, "was to have the boys translate, say, a passage from Cicero and then, a week or so later, put their English versions back into Latin."[8]

"It would seem that a classical education might be rather a poor basis for writing novels in a hard-boiled vernacular," Chandler wrote later. "I happen to think otherwise. A classical education saves you from being fooled by pretentiousness, which is what most current fiction is too full of" (*SL*, 238).

Chandler thought he might become a lawyer, but Uncle Thornton would not pay for the training; instead he proposed a career in the civil service. This had the perquisite of a year in France and Germany, where Chandler would practice the languages in preparation for the civil service exams. "I was a bit passive about the whole thing," he wrote, "since I wanted to be a writer and that would not have gone down at all."[9]

A naive seventeen, Chandler moved to Paris and boarded at a pension on Boulevard St. Michel in the center of bohemian life. He concentrated on learning commercial French at a business college, his only rebellious gesture an interest in esoteric languages such as Hungarian. "I was so innocent," he wrote, "that I didn't realise that there were two girls at the pension that couldn't keep their feet off mine and were offering themselves to my innocence and I never knew it." He was happy "wandering around, with very little money, but a sort of starry-eyed love of everything I saw." Yet Chandler never liked the French; it irritated him that no foreigner could master the language to their satisfaction (*SL*, 407).

After six months Chandler moved to Germany, where he settled in Munich. Rather than attending a school, he worked with a tutor on commercial German. "I did like the Germans very much," he said, "that is, the South Germans. But there wasn't much sense living in Germany, since it was an open secret, openly discussed, that we would be at war with them almost any time now" (*SL*, 250).

Eighteen-year-old Raymond Chandler returned to the suburbs south of London in 1907. With the aid of a former teacher, he began to study for a special civil service exam. He needed to become a citizen in order to qualify. On 20 May 1907 "the Home Office, after a rather perfunctory investigation, simply handed me a Naturalisation certificate." Swearing the oath of allegiance to Great Britain later caused Chandler endless tax and visa problems. The Special Civil Service Exams took place over six days in June 1907. Besides language requirements, which Chandler fulfilled by his residence abroad, the exams demanded advanced knowledge of English, history, mathematics, and Greek. Among the six hundred candidates Chandler placed first on the classics section and third overall.[10]

The prize was a clerkship in the British Admiralty. Raymond Chandler, Assistant Store Officer, Naval Stores Branch, was to keep records on the transfer of naval supplies and ammunition from the naval depots to the fleet stations. His ability with numbers and his rigorous logical abilities made him well suited for the job, and he thought that the easy hours would let him develop his literary career on the side, for many poorly paid literary journalists held government sinecures.

But his temperament conflicted with the job. "I could have had a life-long and perfectly safe job with six weeks' vacation every year and ridiculously easy hours. And yet I thoroughly detested the civil service. I had too much Irish in my blood to stand being pushed around by suburban nobodies. The idea of being expected to tip my hat to the head of the department struck me as verging on obscene," he wrote.

Chandler was also affected powerfully by the suicide of an older writer named Richard Middleton, which he took as an example of the rigors of the literary life. "The incident made a great impression on me, because Middleton struck me as having far more talent than I was ever likely to possess; and if he couldn't make a go of it, it wasn't very likely that I could" (*SL*, 250).

Nevertheless, Chandler quit his job after six months, shocking those who knew him and outraging his Uncle Thornton. His rebellion was designed, clearly, to discover a personal and literary sense of self. "I had grown up in England and all my relatives were either English or Colonial. And yet I was not English. I had no feeling of identity with the United States, and yet I resented the kind of ignorant and snobbish criticism of Americans that was current at that time" (*SL*, 250).

First Attempt at Literary Life

All that Chandler had as evidence of his new career was one poem, "The Unknown Love," which he had published a year earlier in *Chamber's Journal*. The first stanza is typical of the poem's tone, and reveals a romantic streak that surfaces in Chandler's later work:

> When the evening sun is slanting,
> When the crickets raise their chanting
> And the dewdrops lie a-twinkling on the grass,
> As I climb the pathway slowly,
> With a mien half proud, half lowly,
> O'er the ground your feet have trod I gently pass.[11]

"What strikes us in the reading," wrote Jacques Barzun of the poem, "is the recurrent theme of being weighed down by some unnamed tyranny and the equally frequent defiance of it by the heroic ego."[12]

Chandler discovered former Dulwich friends also trying to break into literary life, joined an old boys club, and spent time in Bloomsbury, though he was unaware of the avant-garde writers living there or the literary revolution underway. He lived with his mother still, in an apartment in Streatham, and there was pressure on him to gain real employment.

He worked first as a reporter for the *Daily Express*. "I was a complete flop, the worst man they ever had," Chandler said. "Every time they sent me out on a story I would get lost. They fired me. I deserved it."[13] Uncle Thornton secured him another job at the *Westminster Gazette*, then one of the most influential papers in London. Boss J. A. Spender "was the first editor who ever showed me any kindness," said Chandler (*SL*, 171).

The *Westminster Gazette* was a cluttered paper, composed of news stories, features, poetry, satire, book reviews, political debate, and cartoons. Its most famous contributor was the satirist H. H. Munro, known as Saki. He brought out the Irish inclination toward satire and parody in Chandler and was an important influence.

Deciding to make use of Chandler's abilities in French and German, the editors sent him to the National Liberal Club to read foreign newspapers for items that could be translated for the London audience. These pieces were anonymous, as were the poems Chandler contributed: "I wrote quite a lot of verses for [Spender] also, most of which now seem to me deplorable, but not all, and a good many sketches, mostly of a satirical nature—the sort of thing that Saki did so infinitely better" (*SL*, 249).

The poems that Chandler wrote are similar in form and style, as well as in theme. He wrote in quatrains or sestets with strong, simple rhymes in *abab* pattern. He used archaisms, refrains, and showed no creativity with syntax or enjambment. Of more interest is his use of parallelism, by which he made equal the subjects that he wanted to infuse with romanticism. The first, second, and last stanzas of "The Wheel" are typical:

> The world expends its useless might,
> The heaving nations toil and fight,
> The dizzy thinker peers for light,

> The day doth follow day and night,
>> Is there no rest from anything?
>
> The lover gives another heart,
> The merchant finds another mart,
> The young men have their lives to start,
> The old reluctantly depart,
>> Is there no rest from anything?
> ....
> "Fool! rest shall come when stones can feel,
> Fool! rest shall come when poisons heal,
> Fool! rest comes not at thy appeal,
> Fool! thou art bound upon the Wheel,
>> There is no rest from anything!"[14]

Chandler delighted in presenting the world's diversity as merely an aspect of his central theme, which was moral egalitarianism. "The verse, in short, contains in essence the root idea of all the later tales," wrote Jacques Barzun. Or as Chandler expressed it, "We are all realists at times, just as we are all sensualists at times, all liars at times, and all cowards at times."[15]

Chandler claimed that he landed a job at the *Academy,* a more literary weekly edited by Cecil Cowper, by posing as a potential buyer. Cowper "was not disposed to sell an interest in his magazine, but pointed to a large shelf of books in his office and said they were review copies and would I care to take a few home to review. I wonder why he did not rather have me thrown down his murky stairs" (*SL,* 249).

Between 1911 and 1913 Chandler published twelve essays and reviews in the *Academy.* They are highly critical, concerned with the meaning of writing and being a writer. Chandler was searching for a stance, a persona, a position. He attacked mannered writing in essays titled "The Genteel Artist" and "The Literary Fop" that he later observed were "of an intolerable preciousness of style, but already quite nasty in tone." As Barzun notes, he was guilty of the sins he damned: "Chandler at 23 is in command of his means and enjoys putting things just so."[16]

Chandler also wrote wistfully about the passing of "The Tropical Romance" and "The Remarkable Hero." He wanted romance, but not armchair romanticists. The alternative was realism, but it repelled him. He set the two forces in opposition in "Realism and Fairyland," an essay published in January 1912. Realists, said Chandler "rake over the rubbish-heaps of humanity in its close alleys and noisome slums to find fragments of broken moral crockery, to nose out the vices of unfortunate people, to set upon them the worst possible interpretation for the social system, and, by the simple process of multiplication, to construct from them what they consider typical human beings." He sneered that "of all forms of art, realism is the easiest to practice, because of all forms of mind the dull mind is commonest." Neither scientific inquiry nor its results touched people deeply, said Chandler, because they gave up "intuition and all the soul's fine instincts." The only important writers are idealists because "they exalt the sordid to a vision of magic, and create pure beauty out of plaster and vile dust."[17]

Such phrases as "close alleys and noisome slums," "fragments of broken moral crockery," and "plaster and vile dust" suggest that realism attracted Chandler in spite of his protests. In fact, he incorporated realism liberally in what he called "idealism." He noted that many of the new "realistic" heroes retained the essential romantic characteristic: "The hero may, as far as his social position is concerned, be anybody. He may drop his aspirates, he may be a boor, he may be ignorant of the most elementary rules of polite behavior. . . .But there is one quality which we demand in him: he must be a remarkable person. It matters very little in what his fate lies, whether in art, finance, sport, politics, exploration, swindling, or throat-cutting, but his intellect must be of the cast of great men."[18]

Further in this essay Chandler remarks that the reader "is unaware that the great detective whom he so much admires is as unlike any possible great detective as he is unlike a Patagonian anteater." As this passage suggests, Chandler saw in literary realism new game and preserves in which the "idealist" might go hunting. In this essay and "The Tropical Romance" he suggested that the detective was a generic figure who might benefit from an infusion of his new "idealism."

Chandler's notion of idealism focused on potentiality. For him, the point of realistic technique was not to describe reality or to create "social realism" but to form a base supporting higher possibilities. In one of his last essays for the *Academy*, "Houses to Let," Chandler tried to put his idea into action, describing an old house to which he imparted the radiance of decay. "The effect is like that of a fine etching, colourless but full of suggestion, with a faint flavour of the sordid—but it is the romance of sordidness," he explained. Such phrases as "fine etching. . . full of suggestion" and "the romance of sordidness" hint that Chandler had glimpsed his persona and tone.

Jacques Barzun has shown that Chandler's early work expresses a "hostility to things English, resentment against both convention and corruption, and self-pity over the common lot, mixed with the illusion of self-reliance in the effort to down surrounding evils."[19] In short, Chandler at twenty-three possessed the attitudes that typified his aggressively American essay "The Simple Art of Murder," published thirty years later.

This glimpse of a literary persona was a minor bright spot on the cloudy terrain of Chandler's personal identity. He let it go. He was tired of three guineas a week, of living with his mother and in rented rooms. In a much larger attempt to make manifest his ideals and emotions, Chandler approached Uncle Thornton and asked him for five hundred pounds to go to the United States. "America seemed to call to me in some mysterious way," he said. Over five years, he had published seven articles, twenty-seven poems, and a dozen reviews in addition to some anonymous pieces. Not a great output. Uncle Thornton gave him the loan. "Every penny of it was repaid, with six per cent interest," said Chandler later.[20]

Return to the United States

On board the steamer to New York in 1912 Raymond Chandler met the Warren Lloyds, an upper-middle-class family from Los Angeles with oil money and Ivy League education: they were returning from a year in Germany and shared with Chandler the exile's sense of expectancy on return to his native land. They invited him to visit them in Los Angeles.

When he arrived, Chandler told the customs authorities that he was an American citizen, even though he had "an English accent you could cut with a baseball bat." But he was enthusiastic: "During my year in Paris I had run across a good many Americans, and most of them seemed to have a lot of bounce and liveliness and to be thoroughly enjoying themselves in situations where the average Englishman of the same class would be stuffy or completely bored" (*SL*, 250).

Chandler took the train to St. Louis, where he worked briefly. He did not like the climate or "the great deal of spitting going on," and moved north, to Nebraska, where his Uncle Ernest and Aunt Grace Fitt lived. But life there was too mercantile. So he accepted the Lloyds' invitation: "I arrived in California with a beautiful wardrobe, a public school accent, no practical gifts for earning a living. . . . I had a pretty hard time trying to make a living. Once I worked on an apricot ranch ten hours a day, twenty cents an hour. Another time I worked for a sporting goods house, stringing tennis rackets for $12.50 a week, 54 hours a week" (*SL*, 236).

By the end of his first year Chandler belonged to the Lloyds' social circle. Moving from room to rented room, he used their home as his mailing address. He attended their Friday night "salon," whose guests were united by their interest in parapsychology, Madame Blavatsky, Eastern religions and philosophy. There were also literary evenings, at one of which Chandler coauthored a poem with Lloyd and his daughter Estelle, and musical evenings at which the star was Julian Pascal, a famous West Indian concert pianist who had moved to Los Angeles for his health.

Chandler found a better job after he studied bookkeeping in a night class: "In six weeks the instructor asked me to leave; he said I had done the three years' course and that was all there was." He got a job with the Los Angeles Creamery, which Warren Lloyd, the corporate counsel, found him. Chandler began to track shipments of cream, cheese, and milk. In 1916, when his mother came to live with him, he resided at 311 Loma Drive, in an older neighborhood two miles from downtown L.A. The streets were palm-lined, the houses modest bungalows with small lawns.[21]

In the Lloyd circle it was assumed that Chandler was courting Estelle, the Lloyds' nineteen-year-old daughter. Along with Julian Pascal's son, Gordon, they comprised a circle of the same age. Warren Lloyd, though a good friend, was twenty years older and socialized with the ailing Julian Pascal and his striking wife Cissy. But that was not what happened. A romance developed between thirty-year-old Chandler and the forty-eight-year-old Cissy Pascal, a full-figured, soft-haired beauty who passed for half her age.

The romance was overshadowed when America declared war on Germany in 1917, but it simmered nonetheless. Chandler and Gordon Pascal went to Victoria, British Columbia, to join the Canadian Army. With the pretense of chronicling Gordon's adventures, Chandler wrote Cissy letters. The two young men enlisted in the Gordon Highlanders. After training in Victoria, they sailed from Halifax, Nova Scotia, on 26 November and reached Liverpool ten days later. Chandler was sent immediately to Seaford, on the Sussex coast, where he could see the flicker of bombing and the flash of artillery in France.

In March 1918 Chandler went across the Channel with the Canadian Expeditionary Force, a group that experienced some of the toughest fighting. The German spring offensive skirted the Canadian position on Vimy Ridge, however, and Chandler's unit fell behind the front lines into a reserve position. Eventually they saw dramatic action and Chandler distinguished himself. "If you had to go over the top somehow all you seemed to think of was trying to keep the men spaced, in order to reduce casualties," he later wrote. "It was always very difficult, especially if you had replacements or men who had been wounded. It's only human to want to bunch for companionship in face of heavy fire" (*SL*, 424).

For Chandler the war ended in a sudden barrage of German artillery shells. Everyone else in his unit died; he received only a concussion. "The force of the bombardment hit [me] like the blow of a club at the base of the brain. [I] grovelled against the wall of the trench, nauseated by the din. . . .The sky, in which the calendar called for a full moon, was white and blind with innumerable Very lights, white and blind and diseased like a world gone leprous. . . . [I] began to concentrate on the shells. If you heard them they never hit you."[22]

Chandler was evacuated to Seaford and given a promotion. After he recuperated, he decided to join the Royal Flying Corps with Gordon Pascal and was accepted but never commissioned. In December 1918 he returned to his regiment's London base, and on 20 February 1919 he was discharged in Vancouver with the British war and victory medals.[23]

Chandler was thirty-one years old when he returned, but no closer to stability. He dallied in the Pacific Northwest rather than returning home immediately: "I had another feeble fling at writing and almost sold the *Atlantic* a Henry James pastiche, but I didn't get anywhere." That left business. Chandler didn't want to work in the creamery and thought he might work for one of the English banks in San Francisco. "I think I there for the first time began to dislike the kind of English who don't live in England, don't want to live in England, but bloody well want to wave their Chinese affectations of manner and accent in front of your nose as if it was some kind of rare incense."[24]

Back in Los Angeles, Chandler made another attempt at a literary career, taking a position on the *Los Angeles Daily Express*. But he left after six weeks. He was by now rootless, transient, addicted to greener pastures. He had listed his address during the war as 127 South Vendome St.—Julian and Cissy Pascal's house—and Cissy seemed to be the answer to his peregrinations.

In the liberal circle of the Lloyds and Pascals the affair between Ray- and Cissy, when it became public, was handled in civil fashion. There were discussions. The Lloyds sat down with Cissy, with Julian, with Chandler. Cissy loved Julian, but she loved Ray more. She filed for a California divorce, which was granted in October 1920; but it was four more years until Chandler married her because his mother disapproved of the match. In the interim, Cissy lived in an apartment that Chandler rented in Hermosa Beach, while he lived nearby with his mother in Redondo Beach and later in Santa Monica. Within two weeks of Florence Chandler's death in 1924, thirty-six-year-old Raymond Chandler married fifty-three-year-old Cissy Pascal. It was a union that became the central fact in his life.

Born near Cleveland, Cissy grew up with aspirations of becoming a concert pianist. Exceptionally beautiful, she was both painted and photographed nude as a girl. She met Julian Pascal through her musical connections and married him in 1911 when she was thirty-four. Never orthodox, Cissy lived with a theatrical flair, doing her housework in the nude, dressing conspicuously to highlight her sculptural figure, and dyeing her hair blond. It has been argued that Chandler saw a mother in her. Perhaps he did. But Cissy was educated, wellread, opinionated—a good intellectual companion. She did not look her age and successfully concealed it for years.

Chandler now worked for the Dabney Oil Syndicate, a company owned by Warren Lloyd's brother and Joseph B. Dabney. The Lloyd family owned land in the Ventura Avenue oil fields, while Dabney was a developer from Iowa. Later he sold out to the Lloyds and developed Signal Hill properties that along with neighboring fields once produced 20 percent of the world's oil.

His rise in the oil business was, Chandler said, not as rapid as the growth of a sequoia. The business was expanding and presented opportunities; when a felon was caught in his office, Chandler was promoted. Police arrested the company's auditor for embezzling $30,000, which led to the hiring of an outside auditor from the firm of Haskins, Sells. Chandler was his assistant when the man had a heart attack in the office and died. Chandler accompanied the body to the morgue and witnessed the autopsy, then took over as auditor, and later became vice-president in charge of the Los Angeles office.

Chandler Becomes an Oil Executive

In addition to managing the office staff, Chandler handled all contracts and purchases. He made $1,000 a month, a tremendous amount in the 1920s, and became an executive in the numerous paper holding companies that typified the oil industry. "A director of eight companies and a president of three," he explained, "although actually I was simply a high-priced employe. They were small companies, but very rich. I had the best office staff in Los Angeles and I paid them higher salaries than they could have got anywhere else and they knew it. My office door was never closed, everyone called me by my Christian name, and there was never any dissension, because I made it my business to see that there was no cause for it" (*SL*, 443–44).

As the tone of the passage indicates, Chandler wanted to portray his time at Dabney in a positive light. The facts are darker. Chandler was arrogant and very litigious. He made enemies of principals in the firm, even those related by blood or marriage, and he resisted amiable solutions. He particularly liked to stand up for what he perceived as "right" in legal disputes, rather than to proceed with the "customary" settlement.

I remember one time when we had a truck carrying pipe in Signal Hill (just north of Long Beach) and the pipe stuck out quite a long way, but there was a red lantern on it, according to law. A car with two drunken sailors and two girls crashed into it and filed actions for $1,000 apiece . . . The insurance company said, "Oh well, it costs a lot of money to defend these suits, and we'd rather settle." I said, "That's all very well. It doesn't cost you anything to settle. You simply put the rates up. If you don't want to fight this case, and fight it competently, my company will fight it." "At your own expense?" "Of course not. We'll sue you for what it costs us, unless you pay without that necessity." He walked out of the office.

Chandler hired the best lawyer he knew. They showed that the pipe truck had been properly lighted and then recruited various bar men from Long Beach who testified that the sailors had been thrown out of three bars. "We won hands down," wrote Chandler, "and the insurance company paid up immediately about a third of what they would have settled for, and as soon as they did this I cancelled the policy, and had it rewritten with another company" (*SL*, 445).

Chandler also thought of himself as a human relations expert. When the Board of Directors hired a staff lawyer over his protests, Chandler "found out just how to use his brain, and he said often and publicly that I was the best office manager in Los Angeles and probably one of the best in the world." Chandler's objection had been that the man drank and was unreliable, habits that would soon characterize Chandler.

"Once in a while, not often, I had to fire someone—not someone I had picked myself, but someone who had been imposed on me by the big man [Joseph Dabney]—and I hated that terribly, because one never knows what hardship it may mean to the individual. I had a talent for picking out the capabilities of people. There was one man, I remember, who had a genius for filing. Others were good at routine jobs, but had no initiative. . . .I had to understand them all and use them according to what they were" (*SL*, 444).

At first Chandler ran a superb operation. He impressed secretaries by dictating four-page letters on complex business matters that were clear and, moreover, grammatically flawless. He wrote succinct reports and direct recommendations. He became Dabney's executive assistant, closing deals and resolving details. He began to drive an office Hupmobile in addition to his own Chrysler roadster and moved out toward Beverly Hills. His social circle grew out of his work; he liked to go to USC or UCLA football games with colleagues, to play tennis, or to fly in a rented plane with a professional pilot.

Cissy did not go along on these outings, which were followed by a few social drinks: theirs was a solid marriage, but she avoided situations that exposed her age. At first she dressed stylishly and acted kittenish, decorating her bedroom with pink ruffles. But as she realized that her youthful mascarade was unconvincing, she cited minor ailments to avoid mixing. Chandler socialized by himself.

"He was a loner," said Dabney executive John Abrams. "At the annual oil and gas banquets of 1,000 rollicking oil men at the Biltmore, Chandler was a shadowy figure, stinko drunk and hovering in the wings with a bevy of showgirls, a nuisance." To Abrams, Chandler was a "martinet" who sought to "protect" Dabney "and interfered with field operations and employees."[25]

Irregularities appeared in Chandler's behavior. During one flying session he unfastened his seat belt and stood up in the open cockpit.

He began to drink too much. One Saturday morning he went to play tennis with a friend, but ended up trying to roust the friend's sick wife from her bed. Reprimanded and ordered to leave, Chandler walked into a closet, where he discovered a pistol and pointed it at his head.

He began to disappear from work. Suicide threats became a regular part of the pattern. When his inner cauldron boiled over, he would go off and drink for days at a time, then call up the office to say that he was jumping from a hotel window. Friends ignored him, but the problem grew worse. He started to have affairs with secretaries. A certain secretary began failing to appear on Mondays and was about to be fired when Chandler stepped in and saved her job. It turned out that the two of them had such roaring weekend drunks, in an apartment Chandler rented, that she could not rise until Tuesday and he did not appear until Wednesday. The woman quit on her own.

During this period Chandler wrote a poem, "Nocturne from Nowhere," which reveals a figure that reoccurs in his later fiction. The poem describes a revery:

> In which mingle visions of a woman
> I once loved
> With the visions of a country I have loved
> Almost as well.
>   . . . .
> There are no countries as beautiful
> As the England I picture in the night hours
> Of this bright and dismal land
> Of my exile and dismay.
> There are no women as tender as this woman
> Whose cornflower-blue eyes look at me
> With the magic of frustration
> And the promise of an impossible paradise.
>   . . . .
> So for a little while in the night hours
> Let me go back
> Into that soft and gorgeous future
> Which is not past,
> Never having happened,
> But yet is utterly lost—
>   . . . .
> Into some quiet garden
> Where towards dusk she will come down a path,

Walking as gracefully as a rose sways,
And stop, and with eyes half closed
And a voice a little muted
Say nothing of any great importance.
Only the music of all life and all love
Shall be in her voice,
And in her eyes shall be
Only the light of all youthful love
Which we put away,
With a sort of wry smile,
Knowing there is no such thing,
And if there was,
It would not agree with the urgent necessity
Of making a living.

I do not think I shall touch her hair,
Nor lay groping fingers on her unforgotten eyes.
Perhaps I shall not even speak to her,
But presently turn away, choked with an awful longing,
And go off under the grave English trees,
Through the gentle dusk
Into the land called Death.
And going I shall wonder a little
How much it profits the courses
Of the various sidereal universes
That I could not be permitted to be happy
With the woman I loved
In the land that I loved
For a few brief butterfly hours
Before the deep dark
Came to crown me and anoint me with the opulent splendor
Of oblivion.[26]

More and more often Chandler disappeared. He vanished a week at
a time, and friends could no longer cover his absences. Not even Cissy
knew where he was. When he reappeared, he was irritable and impatient with the details, such as lawsuits, that had been his forte. The
outcome was inevitable but stinging. Chandler got a warning, then
Abrams complained to Dabney, who decided to fire Chandler. In
1932, at the age of forty-four, Raymond Chandler was without work.
It was the cellar of the Great Depression. He had a sixty-two-year-
old wife and a drinking problem. He had been in America twenty

years and gotten nowhere. It "taught me not to take anything for granted," he wrote.[27]

A New Career

Wounded and bitter, Chandler fled up the coast to Seattle, where he had tried to reason out his future after the war. While he was thinking, living with old army buddies, Cissy caught pneumonia and entered the hospital. Chandler returned, packed up his apartment, and moved in with his sister-in-law and her husband. He soon learned that the Lloyds were suing Dabney for misappropriation of the profits from the Ventura Avenue oil fields. When they asked, Chandler gave them everything he could remember about Dabney's dealings; in return the Lloyds gave him $100 a month to help in his new career.

"Wandering up and down the Pacific Coast in an automobile," he explained, "I began to read pulp magazines, because they were cheap enough to throw away and because I never had any taste at any time for the kind of thing which is known as women's magazines. This was in the great days of the *Black Mask* (if I may call them great days) and it struck me that some of the writing was pretty forceful and honest, even though it had its crude aspect. I decided that this might be a good way to try to learn to write fiction and get paid a small amount of money at the same time" (*SL*, 236).

Chandler was a methodical student. He listed himself in the city directory as a writer and enrolled in a correspondence course, completing all of the exercises in narration and dramatic setting that the school sent him. The instructor graded them all A or B+ or B, but Chandler was not the kind of student with whom they usually dealt. He got up in the morning and wrote, or attempted to write, for four hours. "The important thing is that there should be a space of time, say four hours a day at least, when a professional writer doesn't do anything else but write. He doesn't have to write, and if he doesn't feel like it he shouldn't try. He can look out of the window or stand on his head or writhe on the floor, but he is not to do any other positive thing, not read, write letters, glance at magazines, or write checks" (*SL*, 154).

Chandler read the slick and the pulp magazines studiously, dissecting the stories for plot, setting, and characterization. After meeting Erle Stanley Gardner, Chandler wrote to him: "I learned to write a novelette on one of yours about a man named Rex Kane, who was an alter ego of Ed Jenkins. . . . I simply made an extremely detailed synopsis of your story and from that rewrote it and then compared what I had with yours, and then went back and rewrote it some more, and so on. It looked pretty good" (*SL*, 8).

Never a facile writer, Chandler spent five months producing his first story. He never learned to edit; instead he rewrote scenes or stories completely. When he sent "Blackmailers Don't Shoot" off to *Black Mask,* he felt it was perfect. He had even typed it so that the right-hand margin was justified, prompting editor Joseph T. Shaw to comment that he was either a genius or crazy. But it was good material and "Cap" Shaw accepted it. Chandler got paid $180, at the *Black Mask's* basic rate of one penny a word. He finally had himself a career as a writer.[28]

Chapter Two
Life on a Nickel a Word

Black Mask, in which Chandler published his first story, was one of three pulp magazines founded by H. L. Mencken and George Jean Nathan in 1920 to fund their serious magazine, *Smart Set.* But they tired of the field after six months and sold *Black Mask* to their publishers, who hired George Sutton, Jr. and Harry North to edit it. Seizing on Race Williams, a creation of Carroll John Daly, Sutton and North developed the magazine's interest in detective serials.

Race Williams appeared first in a *Black Mask* story of 15 April 1923. He was a detective with a new twist: he was in business for himself, making his living by detection. Unlike Daley himself, who was so absentminded he often could not find his home in White Plains after a trip to New York City, Williams was illiterate, crude, almost subhuman. "I do a little honest shooting once in a while," he said, "just in the way of business [but] I never bumped off a guy what didn't need it." A typical Race Williams story ended on this note: "I sent him crashing through the gates of hell with my bullet in his brain."[1]

Guided by Sutton and North, *Black Mask* writers created more of these tough detectives who were eager to disinfect cesspools of crime. The rise of the magazine to the rank of premier detective pulp, however, was the work of a second editor, Joseph T. Shaw, called "Cap" by his subeditors and writers. Hired in 1926, Shaw was a descendent of blue-blooded New Englanders, a graduate of Bowdoin College, and a national champion in the sabre.

"We wanted simplicity for the sake of clarity, plausibility and belief," Shaw said. "We wanted action, but we held that action is meaningless unless it involves recognizable human character in three dimensional form." Critics have called the style "objective realism," but Shaw's own explanation marches in the opposite direction: he counseled his writers that "in creating the illusion of reality" they should let their characters act and talk tough rather than make them be tough. Shaw's conception of his audience gives a clear indication of the magazine's moral viewpoint. The *Black Mask* reader, he wrote, "is vigorous-minded; hard, in a square man's hardness; hating unfairness, trickery, injustice, cowardly underhandedness; standing for a square deal and a fair show in little or big things, and willing to fight for them; not squeamish or prudish, but clean, admiring the good in man and woman; not sentimental in a gushing sort of way, but valuing true emotion; not hysterical, but responsive to the thrill of danger, the stirring exhilaration of clean, swift hard action—and always pulling for the right guy to come out on top."[2]

Shaw formed this moral outlook after returning to the United States from several years in Europe. He was shocked that the news tabloids celebrated gangsters such as Capone and Dillinger, that scandals rocked the Harding administration, and that Prohibition encouraged ordinary citizens to become minor criminals. The republic appeared more threatened, he said, by corrupt judges, political deals, and institutional sickness than by petty criminals. Shaw's ideology, while overblown and simplistic, overlapped significantly with the English public school training of Raymond Chandler.

Shaw's real coup as editor was to convince Dashiell Hammett, an ailing ex-Pinkerton agent who published stories under Sutton, to write for the magazine again. Early in 1927 Hammet submitted two novellas, *The Big Knockover* and *$106,000 Blood Money,* which he followed with the serialization of his first novel, *Red Harvest.* Not only had Shaw called on Hammett during a period of robust health, but he caught him at his creative peak. In just over thirty months Hammett would publish four of his best works as novelettes in *Black Mask.*

"I doubt that Hammett had any deliberate artistic aims whatever," wrote Chandler, "he was trying to make a living by writing something he had firsthand information about. He made some of it up; all writers do; but it had a basis in fact; it was made up out of real things. . . . Hammett took murder out of the Venetian vase and dropped it into the alley; it doesn't have to stay there forever, but it looked like a good idea to get as far as possible from Emily Post's idea of how a well-bred debutante gnaws a chicken wing."

Much that Chandler saw in Hammett's work he employed and heightened in his own characters: "Hammett wrote . . . for people with a sharp, aggressive attitude toward life. They were not afraid of the seamy side of things; they lived there. Violence did not dismay them; it was right down their street. . . . [He] put these people down on paper as they were, and he made them talk and think in the language they customarily used for these purposes."[3]

Hammett's work showed Chandler not only that there was a distinctly American language and character to be exploited, but that the detective novel did not necessarily have proscribed generic limits. "He demonstrated that the detective story can be important writing. *The Maltese Falcon* may or may not be a work of genius, but an art which is capable of it is not 'by hypothesis' incapable of anything" (*SAM*, 17).

Though he did not publicize his opinion, Chandler also thought that Hammett had weaknesses: his dialogue was not always as good as it could be, and his scenes frequently lacked a sense of necessity and inner luminosity. These were areas in which Chandler was anxious to surpass the younger man.

From "Cap" Shaw Chandler got basic advice on plotting: "To accomplish action it's not necessary to stage a gun battle from start to finish, with a murder and killing in every other paragraph," he said. "You can keep it alive through dialogue."[4] Chandler had great respect for Shaw. He had the "ability to get better writing out of his writers than they could really do," wrote Chandler. Shaw demurred: Chandler "came to us full-fledged; his very first stories were all that could be desired. There was never any question or doubt about Ray's ultimate success."[5]

Chandler's first story, "Blackmailers Don't Shoot," featured a hero named Mallory. "It took me five months to write this thing," said Chandler, "it has enough action for five stories and the whole thing is a goddam pose" (*SL*, 187). His second story, not quite so hyperactive, was "Smart-Aleck Kill." The hero was private detective Johnny Dalmas, who worked in hotels and apartment buildings.

He followed with "Finger Man," and the outstanding "Killer in the Rain," which is told in the first person and became the basis of *The Big Sleep*. " 'Finger Man' was the first story I felt at home with," Chandler wrote. " 'Smart-Aleck Kill' and 'BDS' are pure pastiche. When I started out to write fiction I had the great disadvantage of having absolutely no talent for it. I couldn't get characters in and out of rooms. They lost their hats and so did I. If more than two people were on the scene I couldn't keep one of them alive" (*SL*, 187).

Chandler worked slowly, writing only twenty-one stories over five years. "In the best month I ever had, I wrote two 18,000 word novelettes and a short story which was sold to the *Post*," he wrote (*SL*,

236). But his work improved steadily. He was tough with himself, rewriting far more than contemporaries did. Almost never did he send out the original version of a story. When a story stalled out, instead of editing, Chandler rewrote the whole scene, then adjusted his characters' previous motivations and the mechanics of the plot. The result was a whole new creation, but it cost Chandler much time.

After he had published fifteen stories, Chandler realized that his production method was too slow to be successful in the pulp magazine business, in which writers such as Raoul Whitfield produced thirty stories a year. Even Chandler's friend Erle Stanley Gardner wrote ten thousand words a day. Chandler couldn't do this, so he decided to do what they could not: "The mind which can produce a coolly thought-out puzzle can't, as a rule, develop the fire and dash necessary for vivid writing" (*SL*, 29). He would write novels, with a dash of style.

The Origins of Detective Fiction

Up to this point, Chandler admitted, he had read only three or four mystery novels. Now he began to examine the classics: Conan Doyle, Agatha Christie, R. Austin Freeman, and Dorothy Sayers.

Though *Black Mask* represented a new species of the genre, it was nevertheless in a line of descent running back to the Gothic novel, a form created by an eclectic Englishman named Horace Walpole. His *Castle of Otranto* (1765) had been the foundation of the genre, to which Mary Shelley (*Frankenstein,* 1818) added a scientific aura that evolved into science fiction.

The idea of detection and the figure of the detective were introduced in the nineteenth century by a Frenchman, François Eugène Vidocq. After serving as a soldier, privateer, smuggler, inmate, and secret police spy, Vidocq offered his specialized "security" services to the Paris police. He set up his own department, called the Sûreté, which is the basis of modern French intelligence. When Vidocq published his *Memoirs* in 1828, the book received an English translation the same year. He inspired a number of writers: Jean Valjean in Victor Hugo's *Les Miserables* and Balzac's Vautrin in *Le Père Goriot* derive from Vidocq. Charles Dickens took detail and character from the *Memoirs* for *Great Expectations,* and in America Edgar Allan Poe read and reread Vidocq.

It was Poe who, in stories between 1840 and 1845, framed the detective story as a genre. "The unity of effect of impression is a point of greatest importance," he wrote: "this unity cannot be thoroughly preserved in productions whose perusal cannot be completed in one sitting."[6] Poe's first three "tales" centered on the astounding ability of his sleuth, C. Auguste Dupin. In "Murders in the Rue Morgue" Poe introduced this brilliant detective, whose doings were chronicled by an admiring narrator. Subsequent detectives, notably Sherlock Holmes, became more eccentric, and Poe's amazed narrator turned into Watson and his progeny.

"Rue Morgue" introduced three common detective motifs: the wrongly suspected man, the crime in the sealed room, and the solution by unexpected means. In "The Purloined Letter" Poe invented the plot of the stolen document. In a third story, "The Mystery of Marie Roget," Poe presented the evidence in newspaper clippings, a technique that later attracted the literary realists and prompted Chandler to contrast reality with its newspaper rendering.

By 1870 detective fiction was finding an American audience. Allan Pinkerton published *The Expressman and the Detective* in 1875. Working closer than Poe to the public pulse, Pinkerton never allowed his protagonist the eccentricity that precluded his immediate perception as a "hero." Pinkerton understood that the public was interested in "the immersion of the eye into an almost surreal under-world, an under-world to which he must adapt in order to get his work done." Pinkerton's prose, notes one scholar, "creates an atmosphere of evil commensurate with a sense of the *holiness* of the mission and its necessity for the sanctity of moral order." Pinkerton's next book, *The Molly Maguires and the Detectives* (1877), sketched the modern American detective: "[He] should become, to all intents and purposes, one of the order, and continue so while he remains in the case before us. He should be hardy, tough, and capable of laboring, in season and out of season, to accomplish, unknown to those about him, a single absorbing object."[7]

In England the detective received a more analytic, stylized treatment, best exemplified by the work of Sir Arthur Conan Doyle. His *Study in Scarlet* (1887) introduced the sturdy Watson and the decayed aesthete Sherlock Holmes. Doyle adopted Poe's formulae, cut the elaborate introductions, restated them in crisp dialogue, and emphasized what Poe touched on lightly—the deduction of great conclusions from trifling clues. England produced great masters of this style, such as G. K. Chesterton (*The Innocence of Father Brown,* 1911) and E. C. Bentley (*Trent's Last Case,* 1912).

American detective fiction, however, was influenced by the popularity of dime novels, which drew heavily upon Western frontier locales and heroics that dated back to the Leatherstocking Tales of James Fenimore Cooper. The Beadle and Adams novels, for example, featured versions of the Daniel Boone saga or captivity among the Indians. They introduced such heroes as Indian fighter Seth Jones, the black-clad Deadwood Dick, and universal hero Nick Carter. Among the most popular dime novel "detectives" were Old Sleuth and Old Cap Collier.

The genre experienced an explosion in the 1910s and 1920s with the introduction of mass marketing. This "Golden Era," as critic John Strachey called it, introduced A. A. Milne, Agatha Christie, and Dorothy Sayers to England, while in America Willard Huntington Wright wrote under the pseudonym of S. S. Van Dine about a detective named Philo Vance. The best-selling Vance, Franklin D. Roosevelt's favorite, showed that Natty Bumppo and Sherlock Holmes could be combined. Vance always made sure that justice prevailed, even if as in *The Bishop Murder Case* (1929) he had to engineer a suicide.

The Vance stories appeared in *Scribner's,* one of the respectable "slick" magazines. Writers for these periodicals, such as F. Scott Fitzgerald, earned up to a dollar a word. At the bottom of the scale were the "pulps," published on cheap newsprint, whose writers toiled for a penny a word. Some pulp writers, using a dozen names, produced 1.5 million words a year. "A million words a year is so *usual,*" said one, crediting the invention of the typewriter and noting that previous dime novelists had written seventy thousand words a week in longhand.[8]

The demand for easily read, popular fiction was immense; over twenty thousand magazines were published in 1922. Nearly seventy of these were weekly pulps specializing in romance, flying, Westerns, or detection. Between 1920 and 1950 over 175 different detective magazines graced the newsracks. An aspiring writer could submit to *Girls' Detective, Doctor Death, Speakeasy Stories, Nick Carter Weekly,* or *Argosy All-Story,* each of which offered 150 pages of fiction for ten or fifteen cents. The plots were simple, the characters heroic, the authors plainspoken—it was a mass-produced literature of mass appeal.

To this mass market Raymond Chandler thought he could bring something new—his education, his literary background. A review of the mystery classics may have rounded out his sense of the genre's requirements, but for *writing* he had other models: Henry James, especially *The Spoils of Poynton* and *The Wings of the Dove;* Joseph Conrad's *The Secret Agent;* Merimée's *Carmen* and Flaubert's "Herodias" and "Un Coeur Simple." Dickens and Dumas taught him about characterization; he also read Somerset Maugham, Saki, and Robert Louis Stevenson. Among his contemporaries, except for Hammett, none rivaled the influence of Ernest Hemingway.

Chandler's aim of writing as well as these writers, yet in a popular genre, was complicated by the economic pressures of the epoch. While he was still learning his craft, the subsidy from the Lloyds ended, and the nation slumped into economic depression. Middle-aged, with an aging wife, Chandler felt the pressure and complicated his new career by moving every few months. He disliked his neighbors, or there was too much noise, or the neighborhood was too expensive or too shoddy, or he didn't like the weather. He and Cissy moved again, putting their furniture in storage and living in furnished rooms.

Some years they moved three times. And sometimes they saved money, which was paramount. During the Depression Chandler's income dropped from the $10,000 he earned in the oil business to around $1,000 writing for magazines. His initial rate of payment at *Black Mask* rose from one cent a word to five cents a word, but even in 1938, when he also sold three stories to *Dime Detective,* Chandler earned only $1,275.[9]

Chandler's California

The Los Angeles that Chandler exploited for his settings lay in the shadow, unnoticed by most immigrants. "In a sense it never really existed outside his imagination," said Leigh Brackett, screenwriter of *The Long Goodbye.* Perhaps it took an outsider to see beyond the opportunity, the climate, the pastel landscape, and the palm trees. Chandler was not overwhelmed by California, like most Americans, because he belonged to an English community whose members, while they came for the same reasons as Americans—retirement, good weather, real estate—retained the expatriate's sense of distance. The

English population numbered about eight thousand at the time of
Chandler's arrival and by 1930 had grown to twenty-two thousand.

Over these two decades Chandler witnessed one of the most explo-
sive urban growths in history. The population of Los Angeles County,
just 500,000 when he arrived in 1912, stood at 2.2 million when he
left Dabney Oil two decades later, and continued to increase 11 percent a year for twenty-five years. Most of the migrants were Americans, especially from the Midwest, who came to retire or to find
nonfarm work. Generally middle class, they appreciated the climate
and tracts of single-family housing that spread ever outward. Real estate development was practically the only industry, until the oil and
motion picture industries took hold. Los Angeles had the highest ra-
tio of single-family housing to apartments in the country and publi-
cized the fact: city dwellers came from everywhere to buy a tract
house with an orange tree in the backyard. By 1910 only one fourth
of the population was native.

Initially they pulled together, as settlers do. In 1909 there were
more churches per capita in L.A. than in any other large city in the
nation; all saloons closed on Sunday. The well-heeled population took
an interest in politics, and particularly wanted to avoid the ward system and other evils of eastern cities. They formed a "Good Government" movement and established a strong mayor-city council, a civil
service system, and nonpartisan administrative boards. By 1909 the
Progressives held power, but looked over their shoulders at the Social-
ists, who urged municipal ownership of water and electricity.

Against this background, the crime that did happen looked dramatic to Chandler. But unlike Hammett, who had been a detective,
Chandler had no experience whatsoever with criminals. He learned
about them through the sensational reporting of the newspapers. For
factual accuracy he relied on Major J. S. Hatcher's *Textbook of Firearms*
and Judge Charles W. Fricke's *1,000 Questions Answered for the California Peace Officer*. He did not deign to interview policemen: "Cops
are pretty dumb people," he said.[10] But he did visit his Los Angeles
settings to study them, and his eye for detail made him an acute social observer. He did not take notes, relying on recall at the typewriter.

The most violent era in the city's history occurred just before
Chandler's arrival. When a Socialist victory appeared certain in the
1911 elections, William Randolph Hearst's *Los Angeles Examiner*,
Harrison Grey Otis's *Los Angeles Times* and the city's conservative,

anti-union business interests united to stop them. When two labor organizers bombed the *Times* building and then confessed, the Socialist cause went down to defeat. Events after 1912, the year of Chandler's arrival, "produced extraordinarily uneventful and unenlightened politics," writes one historian.[11]

The conservatives and the Progressives did share some opinions, which Chandler adopted. Chief among them was a prejudice against minorities, especially the Japanese. Opposition to all kinds of Asians became a reflex action for most Californians; separate schools were established and Asians were effectively segregated. Mexicans and blacks, discriminated against by real estate developers, lived in restricted geographic areas. Despite their increasing numbers, minorities were exotic oddities to the white majority, who lived in distant suburbs and seldom saw them.

Prohibition was another issue on which Californians were united. Congress submitted the 18th Amendment to the states in 1917, but California did not get around to passing it until 1919, long after the thirty-six necessary states had done so. Attempts to enforce the law focused on bars and cafes, rather than distillers or bootleggers. The Mexican border and thousands of miles of rocky coastline made smuggling easy. Californians never really took Prohibition seriously: in one bootlegging case the jury was admonished for drinking up the evidence.

Conservatives took the reins in 1922, but Los Angeles politics continued to be dull, though there were numerous national scandals—such as Teapot Dome—during the administration of Warren Harding. Left to its own ideals, the Progressive movement decayed; new residents found profit more attractive than justice, style more important than faith. To an English old boy it was a strikingly slippery moral atmosphere, epitomized by two new industries that were developing: oil and the movies.

Edward L. Doheny discovered oil in Los Angeles in 1892, digging a shaft when he realized that something was percolating up to create the La Brea Tar Pits. Oil soon replaced coal as fuel on the Southern Pacific Railroad, and California became a major market for automobiles when Henry Ford introduced the Model T in 1908. In 1920 Standard Oil discovered a huge oil field at Huntington Beach; the next year Union struck oil near Whittier, and Shell found the biggest field of all—the Signal Hill field at Long Beach, where Dabney Oil was. Scandal plagued the industry, most notably when Secretary of the Interior Albert Fall was convicted of taking a $100,000 bribe from Doheny, but also when C. C. Julian defrauded thousands of Los Angelans with a pyramid scheme that put almost a million dollars in his own pocket. Minor fraud of the sort that Dabney worked on the Lloyds was a daily occurrence.

The motion picture industry came to Los Angeles in 1908 and 1909 to avoid the law back East. Thomas Edison had a patent on the kinetoscope, or movie camera, in the United States, and he prosecuted infringers. The first movies were made in New York, but to avoid Edison's process servers, producers began to travel to the opposite end of the country. When the law appeared, they crossed the border into Mexico.

The moviemakers discovered that Southern California had sunshine and good weather, allowing more shooting days, and locations that could replicate any setting from the Sahara Desert to Sherwood Forest. There is no indication that Chandler was conscious of such pioneers as Mary Pickford, Charles Chaplin, or D. W. Griffith, who worked in Los Angeles in the 1910s; rather he became aware of the medium in the Cecil B. DeMille era (1918–1922), when such pictures as *Forbidden Fruit* began to portray human weakness in attractive terms.

This industry had its own scandals, for its stars lived riotously. Roscoe "Fatty" Arbuckle was accused of crushing a young starlet to death with his massive torso in a San Francisco hotel room. Arbuckle was acquitted, but the Hearst newspapers made a circus of his trial. A few months later Mary Miles Minter and Mabel Normand were linked to the murder of director William Desmond Taylor. Then matinee idol Wallace Reid turned out to be a dope addict. In an effort to impose order, the industry's titans hired Postmaster General Will Hays to become the "Czar of the Movies" and to draw up a moral code. Despite the censorship of the Hays Office, movies found ways to present sex and violence attractively: one of the best, as Chandler no doubt saw, was to describe Sodom and Gomorrah and then allow for their cleansing by a just detective.

Writing *The Big Sleep*

Chandler began to write *The Big Sleep,* a story that uses the oil boom as its background, in the spring of 1938. He knew that some of his short stories had more potential than *Black Mask* permitted him to develop. He took the central plots of "Killer in the Rain," his fourth *Black Mask* story, and "The Curtain," his eleventh, and combined them. He referred to this process, which he used often, as "cannibalizing" his earlier work, and declined to have stories so used reprinted. Chandler wrote *The Big Sleep* in three months, then gave it to Sydney Sanders, an agent used by several *Black Mask* authors. Sanders placed it with Alfred A. Knopf, Inc., which published Hammett's work and other top mysteries in its Borzoi series, a line of books that cost up to two dollars.

When the book appeared and received decent reviews, Knopf urged Chandler to begin a sequel. But Chandler was wary, waiting to see if *The Big Sleep* was successful before he invested more energy. "I have seen only four notices, but two of them seemed more occupied with the depravity and unpleasantness of the book than anything else. In fact the notice from the *New York Times,* which a clipping agency sent me as a come-on, deflated me pretty thoroughly. I do not want to write depraved books. I was aware that this yarn had some fairly unpleasant citizens in it, but my fiction was learned in a rough school, and I probably didn't notice them much" (*SL*, 4).

The sales of *The Big Sleep* were good. The original hardback edition sold ten thousand at $2.00 each, and more in Great Britain, where Hamish Hamilton published it.[12] Before the novel went into paperback, a $1.00 reprint edition by Grosset and Dunlap sold another 3,500 copies. *The Big Sleep* was well received on the West Coast, where reviewers saw its film potential immediately: "There's a very good notice in today's *Los Angeles Times* and I don't feel quite such a connoisseur of moral decay as I did yesterday," wrote Chandler. "They have Humphrey Bogart playing the lead, which I am in favor of also. It only remains to convince Warner Brothers" (*SL*, 4).

Chandler's hardcover earnings on *The Big Sleep* were only $2,000, but he decided to turn his back on the pulps. He had begun to meet fellow writers, exchanging letters and eating with them once a month. The Fictioneers, as they called themselves, were pulp-oriented, but they exchanged information about agents, book publishers, and film studios. Their real purpose, said a member, "was to get comfortably drunk and then en masse attend one of the local burlesque theatres." Among the members were Erle Stanley Gardner, Dwight Babcock, Cleve Adams, and W. T. Ballard, who recalled that Chandler "was a very retiring person who would sit at the dinners after the table had been cleared, sucking on his pipe and offering very little comment. Most writers like to talk about their own work (which is the only reason for a writer's club). Ray seldom did."[13]

Having given up alcohol after Dabney fired him, Chandler may have felt socially sidelined. He drank cup after cup of black coffee, and though affable, he had lost the sense of conversational glide and flow that he gained in the oil business. If the Adamses invited the Chandlers to dinner, Ray remained apart, smoking his pipe. When he visited the Babcocks, he lavished great affection on their cat to avoid talking to them. Sometimes, in order to avoid having his host prepare a meal, Chandler ate at home before he went visiting. He made it clear that he no longer relished the singing, piano-playing, and salon virtuosity of the Lloyds' Friday evenings.

Despite the success of *The Big Sleep,* Chandler remained poor. Sanders urged him to write for the "slick" magazines. "I wrote one story for the *Saturday Evening Post,*" said Chandler, "to placate my agent, who thought I should be a slick writer. The editor liked it, but went on vacation, and his readers rejected it. The rule was then that five readers read a story and one NO knocked it out. When the editor came back, my agent took it up with him, and the editor overruled his readers. To save their faces, I suppose, they asked for a number of changes, and I, being for once in my life a nice little boy, made them. Then they published the story exactly as I had written it."[14]

Members of The Fictioneers regarded the slicks as a corrupting influence, and Chandler agreed with them. "The slicks pay good money and they are very nice people, but the trouble with them is that they are very unsafe. They're never sure what they want and if they guess wrong, you are out of a job. . . .But if you write books, you are not selling your stuff to editors, but to the public. It takes a long time. It's wearing, but when you have the market, you never lose it as long as you can write."[15]

The End of an Era

The *Black Mask* era was ending. The principal contributors held a dinner, which both Hammett and Chandler attended. Hammett was "very nice-looking, tall, quiet, grey-haired, fearful capacity for Scotch, seemed quite unspoiled to me," said Chandler. They all posed for a photo and signed a swatch of tablecloth that they gave to "Cap" Shaw, who was fired shortly afterwards by the magazine's new owner.[16]

That he should know other writers Chandler thought agreeable, but as the friendships grew they involved spouses. Chandler was sensitive about Cissy, who was the foundation of his life; she was aging and infirm. For her health, and to avoid entanglements, the Chandlers began a seasonal transhumance. They moved to Riverside, warmer and drier than Los Angeles, for the winter. They discovered Big Bear Lake (and later Lake Arrowhead), at seven thousand feet in the San Bernardino Mountains and spent the summers there in a rented cabin. In the fall they moved back down to Riverside.

During 1939 the Chandlers discovered La Jolla, and Ray recommended it to friends: "You should look at [it] before you decide where to live. . . . It is dear for a small town, but it has a perfect climate both winter and summer, the finest coastline on the Pacific side of the country, no billboards or concessions or beachfront shacks, an air of cool decency and good manners that is almost startling in California. It has a few writers, not too many, no Bohemian atmosphere (but they will let you take a drink)." But when the Chandlers adopted La Jolla for the winter of 1940, the weather was wet and windy, and Chandler thought he was becoming rheumatic, so they moved to Monrovia, west of Pasadena, and then to Arcadia (*SL*, 7).

"There's a Dead Cat under the House"

Chandler had written to Blanche Knopf that he was twelve thousand words from the end of a book manuscript but had "momentarily mislaid the urge." He wanted to have a title ready for Knopf's spring list, but there was work ahead: "It's rather a mixed-up mess that will run 75,000 words. . . . The title, if you should happen to approve, is *The Second Murderer*. Please refer to King Richard III, Act I, Scene IV" (*SL*, 9–10).

By midwinter Chandler had written himself into a quandary. His journal shows that he worked alternately on *Farewell, My Lovely* and *The Lady in the Lake*. He started *Lady,* stopped to write a short story, continued *Lady* for some pages, then stopped and began *Farewell*. He wrote 233 pages of this novel, then stopped, writing: "This story is a flop. It smells to high heaven. Think I'll have to scrap it and try something new." He wrote a short story, rewrote ninety pages of *Farewell* and again decided he disliked it. So he returned to *Lady,* worked on it steadily, then stopped: "Tragic realization that there is another dead cat under the house. More than three-quarters done and no good" (*SL*, 282–83).

Chandler was also distracted by events in Europe. "The effort to keep my mind off the war has reduced me to the mental age of seven," he wrote. On 29 September 1939 he volunteered for officer's training in the Canadian Army but was rejected. He returned to *Farewell* and pushed forward until he finished a draft. "But if you think I was satisfied with this draft, you are much mistaken, because I rewrote the entire thing in 1940 and finally finished it, although 1940 was a pretty hard year in which to concentrate in view of what was going on in Europe."[17]

There was a dispute about the title. Chandler held out for *Zounds, He Dies:* Mrs. Knopf suggested another Shakespearean title, *Sweet Bells Jangle,* taken from one of Ophelia's speeches in *Hamlet.* They compromised on Chandler's second choice—*Farewell, My Lovely.* Knopf published the hardback in August 1940. Advance sales were disappointing—only 2,900 copies—and Mrs. Knopf blamed the title. Although he got good reviews, a lot of advertising, and high library sales, Chandler felt disappointed. "If this book had sold 10,000 copies, I might have been kidded into the idea that I had a future. As it is I can't help feeling that this particular medium is about the fanciest way of wasting one's talents that I could have hit on." Ten years passed before hardcover sales of the novel reached eleven thousand.[18]

But Chandler cheered when he read reviewer Morton Thompson in the *Hollywood Citizen News:*

I am perfectly willing to stake whatever critical reputation I possess today or may possess tomorrow on the literary future of this author. Chandler writes throughout with amazing absorption in the tasks of craftsmanship. He tries never to miss a trick. His sentences, all of them, show intense effort, constant editing, polishing, never-ending creative activity. His construction is a paradox of smoothness and abruptness of technic. He has a fine taste in story, in drama, and comedy. He employs this sense constantly and he tells his story as well as he possibly can.[19]

In spite of his remark about "wasting one's talents," Chandler was working on several other projects but couldn't finish them. He took up *The Lady in the Lake* again because his summer sojourns at Lake Arrowhead gave him settings. But this novel was a rewrite job, a paste-and-cut remake of a short story, and it bored him. So he began a new novel, which became *The High Window*. When he got tired of either project, he stopped and wrote short stories.

The High Window

Chandler's working title for *The High Window* was *The Brasher Doubloon*. The idea was parodic, continuing a tendency toward burlesque that surfaced in *Farewell, My Lovely*. But domestic moves again interrupted his writing. After five months in Arcadia the Chandlers returned to the San Bernardino Mountains, first to the hamlet of Fawnskin and then to Big Bear Lake, but the town had changed and the Chandlers hated it. They moved to Santa Monica, northwest of Los Angeles, which had a festering shoddiness that had long fascinated Chandler, who used it as a locale for *Farewell, My Lovely* and short stories. Their new apartment was big enough to hold their furniture, which the Chandlers retrieved from storage, but Chandler soon missed the mountain solitude, so they moved farther out, to Pacific Palisades.

Chandler finished a draft of *The Brasher Doubloon* in September 1941, and sent it to Sanders. The manuscript came back with a shocking rejection. Sanders would not even submit it to Knopf. The blow was salutary. Chandler sat down and began to rewrite. The concerted work schedule benefited him, and, despite another move, he finished the revision inside six months. He sent the manuscript back to Sanders but wrote to Mrs. Knopf: "I understand that it is being typed, which seems like a waste of money, and will be submitted to you, and I'm not sure that that is a good idea, but it is out of my hands. At least I felt that you should be relieved of any necessity of being kind to me in a situation where kindness is probably not of any use" (*SL*, 20).

Mrs. Knopf, however, thought *The Brasher Doubloon* was "an absolutely magnificent yarn, beautifully done." As usual, she did not like the title, saying that booksellers would pronounce "Brasher" as "brassiere." A befuddled Chandler wrote back, "I never thought of your idea," explaining that the coin of the title was real, struck in New York City in 1787. Respecting the Knopfs' marketing acumen, he suggested *The High Window* as an alternative: "It is simple, suggestive, and points to the ultimate essential clue."[20]

A minor crisis occurred when the book approached publication. Knopf wanted Chandler's photo on the dust jacket, which amounted to publishing his birthday. "Most writers," Chandler objected, "are such horrible-looking people that their faces destroy something which perhaps wanted to like them. Perhaps I am over-sensitive, but I have several times been so repelled by such faces that I have not been able to read the books without the faces coming between" (*SL*, 21).

The High Window, published 17 August 1942 with the photo, did not sell well. Knopf said that he was disappointed, but Chandler replied that Knopf's own rule of thumb set four thousand hardcover copies as a practical ceiling on the sales of a detective novel. "Either you were just saying that to comfort a broken heart or you are now repining for nothing at all" (*SL*, 22).

In their search for the perfect home, the Chandlers moved next to Idyllwild, in the mountains back of Palm Springs, where they thought the dry climate and altitude would benefit them. Then they moved to Cathedral City, a shabby addition to Palm Springs that Chandler parodied in his letters. Sales of secondary rights to his earlier works were beginning to bring him a constant trickle of money. Within a year Avon published a 25-cent edition of *The Big Sleep* that eventually sold 300,000 copies.

Hollywood was beginning to notice Chandler too. In 1941 Sanders sold the rights to film *Farewell, My Lovely* to RKO Pictures for $2,000. In 1942 Twentieth Century Fox bought rights to *The High Window* for $3,500. It began to look like the lean days might pay off at last.

Chapter Three
Chandler in Hollywood

When he went to Hollywood, Chandler laid aside the manuscript of *The Lady in the Lake,* which he had been working on since 1939. He wanted to see if he could profit by the vogue for detective films that was sweeping Hollywood in the wake of John Huston's successful remake of *The Maltese Falcon.* Ironically, his real acceptance in Hollywood did not come until he finally completed *The Lady in the Lake* four years later.

Sales of this book turned out to be the best of any of Chandler's hardcover publications, establishing him as a novelist in his own right, with a public persona apart from those of Dashiell Hammett and James M. Cain. This especially gratified Chandler, who disliked Cain: "He is every kind of writer I detest, a faux naif, a Proust in greasy overalls, a dirty little boy with a piece of chalk and a board fence and nobody looking. Such people are the offal of literature, not because they write about dirty things, but because they do it in a dirty way" (*SL*, 23).[1]

An invitation to work on the screenplay of Cain's *Double Indemnity* was the bait, however, that drew Chandler to Hollywood. Billy Wilder suggested the Cain novelette to a Paramount producer who was a detective-novel fan, and he found Chandler's address through Knopf. To Chandler the call from Hollywood signaled the beginning of the big time: hadn't Dashiell Hammett gone to Hollywood after his work became popular? In his eagerness to get on with fame Chandler volunteered to write the screen treatment for a few hundred dollars. Too professional to exploit him, the producer sent Chandler to H. N. Swanson, an important Hollywood agent. To Chandler's astonishment, he ended up getting $750 a week for thirteen weeks.

Chandler went to work in the fabled Paramount Writers Building, which was built around a courtyard and called both the "Campus" for its collegiate ambience and "The Tower of Babel" because of the emigré writers there. At first he did not like the plain offices and nine-to-five schedule. Billy Wilder, his coauthor, sent Chandler home with *Double Indemnity* on Friday: on Monday Chandler returned with an almost complete screenplay, including lighting directions and camera angles. Wilder himself had just done a few pages. Working with Wilder, said Chandler, "was an agonising experience and has probably shortened my life; but I learned from it as much about screen writing as I am capable of learning, which is not much."[2]

Wilder and Chandler wanted to preserve as much of the original, especially the dialogue, as they could. But they found the lines stilted when spoken. "Nothing could be more natural and easy and to the point on paper, and yet it doesn't quite play," wrote Chandler to Cain (*SL,* 28). So Chandler rewrote the dialogue. When the script of *Double Indemnity* was nominated for an Academy Award, Wilder gave the credit to Chandler, "one of the greatest creative minds" that he had encountered. The success of the movie and the nomination made Chandler's reputation in Hollywood.

Originally Chandler had planned to take the money and run. He and Cissy moved back out to the desert, where Chandler wanted to start a new novel; he told Alfred Knopf that it would concern the wealthy set of Bel Air, three men and two women, and wouldn't be a mystery. But there were problems. "I was so completely pooped after nine months at Paramount that I couldn't even make myself write a letter. Just sat and stared morosely out of the window at the sand dunes" (*SL,* 27).

When Chandler recovered, he returned to Hollywood, installing Cissy in a large house in the Fairfax District. They took their furniture out of storage again, but otherwise lived far below their means. Chandler didn't plan on entertaining: "Most movie people are fine to work with, but I don't like to go into their homes, don't like to listen to the same old talk—pictures and more pictures. Furthermore, I don't want their scale of living, and if you don't live as expensively as they, well, you just don't belong."[3]

But he grew to like the easygoing atmosphere of the Writers Building. They went to work around ten and took eight months to write a screenplay. Coffee, liquor, and food were available at the switchboard, but best of all was the company. "At the writers' table at Paramount I heard some of the best wit I've heard in my life," Chandler said. "Some of the boys are at their best when not writing."[4]

His new contract called for Chandler to work on scripts that were under way and needed help. He collaborated with Frank Partos on

And Now Tomorrow and with Hagar Wilde for *The Unseen*. Toward the end of his contract Chandler began to succumb to his personal nemeses: a producer strong-armed him into Lucey's, a fancy bar across from the studio, and got him drunk. The actresses and secretaries at the studio flustered Chandler, and he began to mourn his lost youth; increasingly there was a bottle in his drawer and a young woman to help him. During an affair with one secretary he disappeared for several weeks. As a makeup present, he bought his seventy-three-year-old wife a Lincoln sedan that was too big for either of them to drive.

The Simple Art of Murder

When his contract expired in September 1944, Chandler went home to write, leaving the arrangement of a new contract to his agent. Knopf had sold *The Big Sleep* to Warner Brothers and Chandler's share came to $7,000. With this and money he saved (Chandler bought government bonds with his movie money) he could afford to write. But it was an article for the *Atlantic* on the detective novel, rather than his projected novel, that claimed Chandler's attention. His essay "The Simple Art of Murder" became a classic.

The first day of 1945 found Chandler, in high spirits, writing that "I regret to say that I have to go back to work tomorrow. The prospect makes me feel low enough to chin myself on the curbing." He had a new three-year Hollywood contract that mandated twenty-six weeks of work a year, beginning at $1,000 a week and rising thereafter. As a perquisite, his first assignment was an original screenplay (*SL*, 40).

Chandler plunged into his new assignment. He had a story that he thought could be produced as a movie, and he set about converting it. "In less than two weeks I wrote an original story," he said. "All dictated and never looked at until finished" (*SL*, 46). The producers loved it, and since they wanted to rush their highest-paid actor, Alan Ladd, through a film before he was drafted, they put Chandler's script into production. Then he realized he was in trouble: "they are already casting it, without a line of screenplay written. Why do I get myself into these jams?"[5]

Director George Marshall caught up with Chandler's script and the studio got nervous. The production chief called in Chandler and offered a $5,000 bonus if he could finish on time. Chandler was insulted. He consulted producer John Houseman, an old boy and fellow

Englishman, about the "bribe" to finish the contracted work. Chandler wanted to quit then and there, but he realized that would put Houseman in a tough spot—and a public school man did not do that to a friend. Chandler said he could complete the script only in a continuous alcoholic siege.

Houseman arranged for Paramount to provide two limousines to stand by outside Chandler's house. They would get the doctor for Cissy, take the maid shopping, and run the script to the studio. There were round-the-clock nurses for Cissy and a doctor who gave Chandler vitamin shots, since he never ate while drinking. Secretaries had to be present at all hours for typing and dictation. A direct telephone line was installed between the house and Paramount.

Then Chandler and Houseman went to Perino's Restaurant, where Chandler had three double martinis before lunch and three stingers after. Houseman drove him home. The limousines and secretaries were in place. Chandler worked intermittently during the next week, never out of control, but always in another world. Houseman would see him slumped over the dining room table, passed out or asleep, then he would wake up and continue drinking and writing. In the evenings he listened to music on the radio with Cissy. Then he would write a few more lines before nodding off again. But he finally finished the screenplay, including all the revisions required by the producer.[6]

In the final analysis, Chandler would have done better to have saved his health. His script became *The Blue Dahlia,* but alterations reduced the distinctive Chandler touch to sections of dialogue. The Navy objected to the story line, which concerned a brain-damaged medical corpsman, so changes in the plot removed its subtleties. Then the studio and his agent urged Chandler to write what is now called a "novelization" of the movie. The *Saturday Evening Post* would serialize it in six installments. But Chandler turned them down, complaining of weariness and ill health.

It was a period of disintegration. Chandler wanted to write another Marlowe novel, but Hollywood tempted him with lucre. He renewed his friendships with the bottle and young ladies from the office. The *Atlantic* badgered him to write articles, his agents to write stories for the slicks. MGM bought rights to *The Lady in the Lake* and asked Chandler to write the screenplay. They implied that if he didn't, someone else would, and not in the fashion he wanted. Paramount had no prohibitions against his working for a rival temporarily, so

Chandler went. Deciding that the rewrite was boring, he began to reinvent the story; but the producers and director complained that they wanted the original. Chandler didn't finish inside his deadline, leaving behind a partial script and refusing a screen credit. "Probably the worst movie ever made," he said, "after that one was over I had to be hit on the head with a baseball bat to make me get up out of a chair."[7]

While his agent sought a new contract, Chandler took Cissy to Big Bear Lake and rusticated. Discussions between the agent and the studios focused on ways Chandler could work without cracking up. He could be paid a flat fee, without deadlines. He could become a writer-director like Wilder. He could become a producer. Chandler turned down all suggestions: he no longer needed the money. In fact, he had paid $50,000 in income taxes in 1945.

"One of the troubles is that it seems quite impossible to convince anyone that a man would turn his back on a whopping salary—whopping by the standards of normal living—for any reason but a tactical manoeuvre through which he hopes to acquire a still more whopping salary. What I want is something quite different: a freedom from datelines and unnatural pressures, and a right to find work with those few people in Hollywood whose purpose is to make the best pictures possible within the limitations of a popular art" (*SL*, 63).

"Out of the Business"

What Chandler really wanted was out of the business, but after years of poverty he couldn't bear to part with the cushion. He denounced "Writers in Hollywood" in the *Atlantic* in a deliberate attempt to distance himself from the film community, and he did find it cooler toward him afterwards. Charles Brackett, another writer, quipped that "Chandler's books are not good enough, nor his pictures bad enough, to justify that article."[8]

But Chandler did enjoy consulting on Howard Hawks's version of *The Big Sleep*. William Faulkner and Leigh Brackett were the scriptwriters, Humphrey Bogart the star. Chandler talked with them and planned a new (but unused) ending with Hawks. The release of *The Blue Dahlia* brought Chandler an Edgar from the Mystery Writers of America and an Academy Award nomination for the screenplay.

Chandler had recommended La Jolla to friends, and Cissy liked it. In 1946 they moved to 6005 Camino de la Costa, a new corner house overlooking the ocean. The price was $40,000: Chandler's gift to his seventy-six-year-old wife for having endured the migrations, the Dabney Oil epoch, and then Hollywood. "We have a much better home than an out-of-work pulp writer has any right to expect," he wrote (*SL*, 79).

Chandler knew a few people in La Jolla, writers with whom he played tennis, but he had little social life because of Cissy's illnesses and retiring nature. He gave up alcohol again, and was uncomfortable when guests stopped by, but at least he was far from the temptation of young women. He began to blend into the "arthritic billionaires and barren old women" of La Jolla, establishing routines that persisted until Cissy's death.[9]

He rose early and went to his study, working there until noon, when he joined Cissy for lunch. After lunch, dressed in a jacket and tie, he would read or drive his Oldsmobile to the business district of La Jolla to do chores. He returned by four p.m. to take tea with Cissy. A series of hired cooks prepared dinner (never to Chandler's satisfaction) after which Cissy played the piano or they listened to records. Cissy went to bed early; then Chandler began to read and to dictate letters, a process that lasted until after midnight.

Free of the studios and the necessity of producing to support himself, Chandler's tendencies to procrastination and perfectionism grew. He interested himself in his critical reputation, the status of the detective novel, and his myriad correspondents, answering requests for biography and accusations of anti-Semitism. He wrote articles for the *Atlantic* and thought about the possibilities of film. All of this prevented progress on the novel that he wanted to write.

Chandler was also afraid that Hollywood had ruined his talent for fiction and he was bored with Marlowe, although he said that "for business or professional reasons I think the guy is too valuable to let die out. But I find myself spoofing more and more."[10] He completed half of the new novel, to be called *The Little Sister,* and sent it to his agent on 1 June 1948. "Please bear in mind that this material was all dictated to a dictaphone, an instrument which I have found very convenient for movie work, but I am not sure it is adapted to fiction writing" (*SL*, 118).

When he finished the book in September, Chandler hoped it would be the last Marlowe story. His English publisher put it into production immediately, and his New York agent sold an abridgment to *Cosmopolitan* for $10,000. The book was an attempt to reveal Hollywood as it was; Chandler admired Nathanael West's *The Day of the Locust* and F. Scott Fitzgerald's *The Last Tycoon.* But his attempt to achieve that stature fell flat, revealing how moviemaking had changed Chandler. He used research he had gathered in 1945 to prepare *The Blue Dahlia,* but neither in plot nor theme did he surpass his previous work.

Sales of *The Little Sister* were respectable. Hamish Hamilton sold 26,000 hardback copies in England, while Houghton Mifflin eventually sold 16,000 trade editions in the United States. Chandler received $10,000 for the work in hardback. Widely reviewed, the book earned praise and considerable criticism. The *New York Times Book Review* said it demonstrated a "scathing hatred of the human race."[11]

Encroaching Illnesses

Chandler might have been more concerned had not his own and Cissy's illnesses preoccupied him. He developed a skin allergy that split his fingertips and a rash which, as it spread over his neck and chest, he needed morphine to withstand. He had to bandage his fingers to type and wear gloves to read. Then he developed shingles; meanwhile a chronic lung condition enfeebled Cissy.

Chandler blamed everything on La Jolla. He railed against the cost of living, the inclement weather, and the energy he lost taking care of business. But it was really the neglect of his life with Cissy that irritated him; he was preparing himself psychologically for her death. He began to do the things he had always planned to do with her. At the top of the list was travel to England, but Cissy's condition worsened and they postponed that. Instead they traveled to Palm Springs and then to a dude ranch in the Santa Ynez Valley.

To keep the income flowing, Chandler and his agents promoted television and radio shows based on Philip Marlowe. Chandler never made the money from these that Hammett, Gardner, or Spillane did, but he drove hard deals. He received proposals for anthologies, wrote another article for the *Atlantic,* then signed on at $2,500 a week to write a script for Warner Brothers, to be produced by Alfred Hitchcock.

Hitchcock and Chandler did not get along. As Hitchcock recalled, "We'd sit together and I would say 'Why not do it this way?' and he'd answer, 'Well, if you can puzzle it out, what do you need me for?' " Chandler referred to Hitchcock within his hearing as "that fat bastard." The director had an assistant rewrite Chandler's script of *Strangers on a Train*. Though he shared credit, Chandler was humiliated by the hamhanded rewriting and by the film's great popularity. He took out his ire in "A Couple of Writers," a parody of Hollywood that his agent sent around to magazines for almost a year without result. [12]

During 1950 Chandler worked in bits and stretches on a new novel that he called *Summer in Idle Valley*. By the fall of 1951 he had written 50,000 words. In October he wrote to Hamish Hamilton, "I hope to have a book in 1952, I hope very hard. But dammit I have a great deal of trouble getting on with it. The old zest is not there. I am worn down by worry over my wife. . . .I wake in the night with dreadful thoughts. Cissy has a constant cough which can only be kept down by drugs and the drugs destroy her vitality" (*SL*, 291). Later that month Chandler read the manuscript through and disliked it. "Have enough paper written to make it complete," he wrote his agent, "but must do all over again. I just didn't know where I was going and when I got there I saw that I had come to the wrong place" (*SL*, 295–96).

Six months later Chandler felt that he was done. He sent his typescript to Bernice Baumgarten at his agents, Brandt and Brandt: "I'm sending you today, probably by air express, a draft of a story which I have called *The Long Goodbye*. It runs 92,000 words. I'd be very happy to have your comments and objections and so on. . . .I wrote this as I wanted to because I can do that now" (*SL*, 314–15).

Bernice Baumgarten and her boss, Carl Brandt, read the manuscript immediately. Brandt wrote a three-page memo criticizing a number of minor things and the "Christlike" character of Marlowe. Baumgarten repeated the same points in her note: "We feel that Marlowe would suspect his own softness all the way through and deride it and himself constantly." [13]

Chandler was stunned. He cabled them to not copy the manuscript, not to send it to Hamish Hamilton: "I regret having sent the script out when I did. I was just too impatient to get rid of it. I knew the character of Marlowe had changed, and I thought it had to because the hardboiled stuff was too much of a pose after all this time. But I did not realize that it had become Christlike, and sentimental, and that he ought to be deriding his own emotions. It may be that I am no good any more. God knows, I've had enough worry to drive me off the beam" (*SL*, 315).

He began to revise immediately. But he did as he wanted, not changing the character of Marlowe so much as making it consistent. He rewrote the end twice, attempting to retain his commentary on friendship while avoiding sentimentality. "There is no doubt that Chandler intended to put all of himself into *The Long Goodbye*," writes his biographer. "He knew it was his last chance to do so."[14]

Final Business

The revisions were not quite finished when Chandler embarked on the long-planned trip to London with a frail, ill Cissy. Six months earlier he had written to Hamish Hamilton, "I dread, and I am sure she does . . . a slow decline into invalidism. . . .I feel the icy touch of despair" (*SL*, 292). The Chandlers prepared as though for a safari. They fussed over food, over clothes, and over accommodations. Once en route, they didn't like New York, they didn't like the *Mauritania*, their ship. In London, they complained about the prices, their hotel, their towels, and their lost luggage.

Yet, for Chandler, it was a return to the land that had formed him, an overdue reacquaintance with social milieus he had valued above those of America. In the end, he wrote, "We loved London and we had a lovely time there. What little inconveniences we happened to have suffered were all due to our own inexperience and probably would not happen again. . . .people were wonderful to me. It really was extremely touching" (*SL*, 326).

Chandler took up his revisions of *The Long Goodbye* when he returned, but did not finish until midwinter. Cissy had sprained an ankle in London, got an infection, and become bedridden. Her sister came to help, but Christmas celebrations were scrapped. Meanwhile, Chandler fired Brandt and Brandt for what he felt was their tactless treatment of him. He had discovered the gimlet, a cocktail made of gin and lime juice, aboard the *Mauritania*, and began to drink one with Cissy every evening—his first drinking in six years. He finished *The Long Goodbye* in July, sending it off to Hamish Hamilton and later to Houghton Mifflin. Hamilton published a first run of 25,000 copies, and in March 1953 Houghton Mifflin printed another 15,000 hardback. The reviews were very good.

It was just as well that no writing projects remained on Chandler's table, for Cissy deteriorated rapidly. He took her to a lung specialist in San Diego, then to the Scripps Clinic in La Jolla, and finally to a

specialist in Los Angeles. The diagnosis was fibrosis of the lungs, a
hardening that begins at the bottom and spreads upwards, gradually
strangling its victim.

> By December 7th, I realized she was dying. In the middle of the night
> she suddenly appeared in my room in her pajamas looking like a ghost, hav-
> ing evaded the nurse somehow. . . .At three A.M. on the morning of De-
> cember 8th her temperature was so low that the nurse got frightened and
> called the doctor, and once more the ambulance came and took her off to the
> hospital. She couldn't sleep and I knew it took a lot of stuff to put her under,
> so I would take her sleeping pills and she would tie them in the corner of
> her handkerchief so that she could swallow them surreptitiously when the
> nurse was out of the room.
> ....
> Of course in a sense I had said goodbye to her long ago. In fact, many
> times during the past two years in the middle of the night I had realized
> that it was only a question of time until I lost her. But that is not the same
> thing as having it happen. Saying goodbye to your loved one in your mind
> is not the same thing as closing her eyes and knowing they will never open
> again. But I was glad that she died. To think of this proud, fearless bird
> caged in a room in some rotten sanitarium for the rest of her days was such
> an unbearable thought that I could hardly face it at all. . . . For thirty years,
> ten months and four days, she was the light of my life, my whole ambition.
> Anything else I did was just the fire for her to warm her hands at. (SL, 378–
> 79)

Although they knew almost no one in La Jolla, Chandler wanted
Cissy to have a large funeral. It was held in the nave of St. James
Episcopal Church, but only ten people showed up. Chandler, who
had been drinking, took the group back to his house, where they
drank more. "I see a gentle smile hovering at the edge of the lamp-
light and I hear a voice calling me by a pet name," he wrote. "Then
I go out to the pantry and mix a stiff brandy and soda and try to
think of something else" (SL, 379).

The memories led to depression, the depression to self-pity. Chandler began to threaten suicide. He phoned the police and told them
they would find his corpse on the floor, then called a friend in London
to repeat the threat. In February, however, he got a gun, locked himself in his bathroom, and fired two shots. When police arrived, they
found the drunk, somewhat pleased Chandler gazing at a bullet hole
in the ceiling.

"I couldn't for the life of me tell you whether I really intended to go through with it or whether my subconscious was putting on a cheap dramatic performance," said Chandler. His attempt made the newspapers though, and letters of sympathy and support poured in. Chandler didn't read them: he had lost himself so thoroughly in alcohol that his housekeeper sent him to the county hospital.[15]

It was the beginning of a long, final battle with the bottle. Chandler tried to rally: he checked out of the hospital, sold his house, and bought a train ticket to New York City, planning to sail for Britain. But as he waited at the Waldorf for the *Mauritania's* departure, he began to drink, ending up in New York Hospital to dry out. Released and installed in a new hotel, he called friends to threaten suicide again.

Life in London

On 12 April 1955 Chandler sailed for Southampton, determined to begin a new life: he had friends in London and a new novel, *Playback*, to finish. During the journey he learned that he had won an Edgar from the Mystery Writers of America for *The Long Goodbye,* which was judged the best mystery of the year. He also met Jessica Tyndale, an American representative of an English bank, for whom Chandler fancied himself a kind of chaperon. When he arrived in England he was already in the role of gallant and bon vivant that he was to assume for the remainder of his life. He telegrammed a friend: "Don't meet. Have woman with much luggage."[16]

The new life took time to coalesce, however, and in the interim Chandler resumed drinking. Now a well-known literary figure, he was introduced to Stephen Spender and his wife, Natasha, to Ian Fleming, to Sonia Orwell, and to journalists and intellectuals. They found his California suits, the yellow gloves he wore to protect his fingers, and his American slang very picturesque. Alternately numb from alcohol and embarrassed, Chandler attempted to live up to his new role.

Gradually he became what they expected: a character from one of his novels. He made the similes that he put once in Marlowe's mouth, he told jokes that convulsed the room, he became a fleshy, silver-haired celebrity. "You go to luncheon with eight people and next day five of them invite you to a dinner party," he said. "So dine, drink and drab is about all you do."[17]

Filling the role took its toll. Chandler failed to show up at parties in his honor, including one attended by Noel Coward and Somerset Maugham. He drank excessively, but feared meeting celebrities unless he was well lit. He was thrown out of his hotel for having a woman in his room. His concern for these "girl-friends" became mawkish and exaggerated. An infatuation with Natasha Spender led him to propose a trip to Italy, which she accepted to keep him from drinking himself to death.

In the fall of 1955, when Chandler's six-month visa expired, he returned to California, but only briefly. He became homesick for London and six weeks later returned on a night flight over the North Pole. He found that Natasha Spender had to have an operation and proposed to her husband that she rest up for it with him in Madrid and Tangier. The Spenders agreed, thinking Natasha would check Chandler's drinking. The trip rejuvenated Natasha, but by Christmas Chandler was lost in the bottle again.

He rented a flat near the Spenders, hoping that eventually he could persuade Natasha to move in with him. Then he discovered that the Spenders wanted to incorporate him into their family: to their children he would be kindly, silver-haired Uncle Ray. Unable to make reality conform to his hopes, he overstayed his visa, leaving the country under the threat of punitive taxes in May 1956.

Back in New York City he attached himself to Jessica Tyndale, but his drinking was so severe that he was committed to New York Hospital and required transfusions for sixteen hours. It took him until June to recover. Then he returned to La Jolla, but was hospitalized again. With the arrival of his new agent, Helga Greene, from London, Chandler actually wrote a little. Working in Palm Springs, he finished *Playback,* which he had promised to Houghton Mifflin for April 1958.

Playback Published

"By getting up at 6 a.m. and working ten hours straight with no food but coffee and Scotch I finished the Marlowe book," he wrote. He sent the typescript to Houghton Mifflin in December 1957. Helga Greene's presence cheered Chandler, but sales of the new novel were disappointing, only 9,000 copies in the United States. Fans disliked the change in Marlowe's character, and *Newsweek* ran a story on the "soft-boiled detective" who liked the police. Chandler worried, but was soon preoccupied by more serious matters.[19]

His London lawyer informed Chandler that the British were charging him income taxes for overstaying his visa in 1955; furthermore they weren't recognizing his naturalization as an American citizen. It was a nuisance suit, quickly settled by a decree in the U. S., but Chandler got caught in a voluminous correspondence with his agents, publishers, lawyers, and government officials.

In 1958 he returned to London, settling near Helga Greene. But he found that she could not give him full-time attention, and he had emotional baggage—his ex-secretary and her children in California—that resulted from and yet exacerbated his loneliness. The only solution was activity, and Chandler tried to keep busy. The *Sunday Times* asked him to interview Lucky Luciano in Italy: the prospect of America's most famous crime writer interviewing America's most famous criminal intrigued them. Chandler went, but the interview was flat: Luciano remembered Chandler as a "swell guy."[20]

During 1958 Chandler adopted a sober regimen; a male nurse established routines in his life, making sure that he ate and slept regularly. During the day he wrote letters, explored the creation of a tax shelter in the Bahamas, and played darts. He became the model expatriate man of letters. To Helga Greene he wrote, "my home is in Europe. For some reasons, perhaps you, I have grown away from the American attitude to life. Americans are kindly and generous people, vital and energetic, but no cachet. I'd rather have decadence with style, if I have to have it, rather than crudeness."[21]

Back to La Jolla

In the fall of 1958 he returned to La Jolla to attend to the problems of his ex-secretary, for whom he had become a financial Sir Galahad. Installing himself in a cottage in the center of town, Chandler tried to work on a Marlowe story that he titled "The Pencil." It was clear to his agent, however, that he could no longer live alone, so she dispatched his housekeeper from London.

Chandler returned from the clinic, when he was again drying out, to find such an intense rivalry between the ex-secretary and the housekeeper that the latter had to be hospitalized for rest, which she dutifully reported to Helga Greene, who was herself ill in the London

Clinic. Thus began a tawdry battle to be named Chandler's heir. Apparently conscious that he was dying, Chandler updated his will regularly, changing the beneficiary back and forth.[22]

In February 1959 Helga Greene flew to California and committed Chandler to the La Jolla Convalescent Hospital. A doctor told him he could not live more than five months. "He's a liar," said the writer, "I'll live forever." By March he recovered enough to go to New York with Greene to accept the presidency of the Mystery Writers of America. To spare him the emotional confusion of La Jolla, Greene registered Chandler in the Beaux Arts Hotel on East 44th Street, where Jessica Tyndale lived. But the inclement weather gave him a cold, and the ex-secretary wrote him pathetic letters about her problems.

Chandler returned to La Jolla and, finding that his old cottage had not been rented, moved back in. He began to drink before he had conquered the cold, and on 23 March entered the La Jolla Convalescent Clinic, suffering from pneumonia. Two days later he was transferred to the Scripps Clinic, where he died on the afternoon of 26 March 1959.

Chapter Four

Looking for a Knight:
The Short Stories

Before he invented Philip Marlowe in *The Big Sleep,* Chandler created prototypes in gambler Johnny De Ruse, policeman Sam Delaguerra, vice detective Pete Anglich, hotel dick Steve Grayce, and man-about-town Ted Malvern. His best effort was a private detective named Mallory, after the author of *Le Morte d'Arthur.* Later Chandler changed his name to Carmady, and finally to John Dalmas.

Mallory appears in Chandler's first story, "Blackmailers Don't Shoot" (*Black Mask,* December 1933). While the story is primitive compared to his later efforts, and flawed by clichéd dialogue, motiveless actions, and pointless turns of plot, it was relatively polished by *Black Mask* standards.

Private detective Mallory comes to Los Angeles from Chicago, Chandler's birthplace, at the request of a gambler named Landry. His love letters to former girlfriend and film star Rhonda Farr have been stolen. The blackmail becomes kidnapping when a gang of crooked cops, politicians, and crooks, led by her own lawyer, snatch Farr and Mallory. He escapes, turns the tables by kidnapping the lawyer, then frees Farr while the gang members kill each other. In the resolution Mallory learns that Farr set everything in motion; her contract was expiring and she wanted publicity. That fed Landry's vindictiveness and her attorney's greed; they conspired against her with the gang. At the story's end, a policeman tells Mallory that Eclipse Films needs a detective.

Blackmail and kidnapping became Chandler's favorite plots. Blackmail threatens the public image of a person, which is usually a charade anyway, and kidnapping removes the actual person, putting his worth to others in question. The motive for both crimes is money, the desire for which causes all evil in Chandler's early work. He also experimented with the captivity of the heroine or detective, a time-tested device of American melodrama that originated in Puritan nar-

ratives of captivity among the Indians. In this early work the Indians
are clearly criminal. Later on, the tendrils of drugs and gambling lead
from the criminals to Hollywood, providing Chandler with a canvas
that encompasses society and giving his detective grounds for sweeping moral judgments.

This first story also employs a plot pattern to which Chandler
turned repeatedly: a triangle in which two men love one woman who
manipulates both of them. One of the men hires or is a friend of the
detective; in this man's demise the detective sees his fate if he had
loved the woman. In later work the detective himself becomes part of
the triangle.

Chandler featured Mallory, renamed Dalmas in later editions, in
his second story, "Smart-Aleck Kill" (*Black Mask*, July 1934). Now
employed by Eclipse Studios, Mallory tries to help smut director
Derek Walden find out who is blackmailing him. Two thugs kidnap
Mallory and by the time he returns, Walden is dead, an apparent suicide. He learns that Walden liked liquor and supplied himself, during Prohibition, by smuggling booze from Ensenada. This left him
open to blackmail by gangsters; he turned for protection to a gang
run by Councilman John Sutro and racketeer Gay Donner. Sutro kills
Walden, then Donner, and is killed in turn by his wife for having
had an affair.

Why does Sutro kill Walden? Loose plot ends and improbable mo-
tives mar this story. It uses Prohibition-era settings and rationales,
but Prohibition (1920–33) ended before it was published. Most of the
characters are stereotyped, their lines predictable, and their reactions
mere generic conventions. Some minor touches are notable, such as
the portrait of Helen Dalton, first in a series of blonde bitches, and
the dialogue sometimes reveals an acute ear, such as Denny's line: "I
don't what you call know him." There are also indications, such as
Mallory's "We gotta find out all about it before the cops even know
Walden is dead. . . . Like they do in the movies," that Hollywood
was not just a setting for Chandler, but an influence and a goal from
the start. According to the editors of *Black Mask*, their magazine was
"regarded by the biggest motion picture companies as one of the important sources of new story material. . . . three of our series heroes
are very much in the mind of the film producers at this time."[1]

Like his first two efforts, "Finger Man" (*Black Mask*, October
1934) involves a corrupt politician who deals in influence and blackmail. "I'm tough and I get what I want," says Frank Dorr. Chandler's

now nameless detective unravels the fabric of politics and crime behind Dorr's organization, but the story lacks significant tensions and female characters. Nevertheless, Chandler felt that he hit his stride with this story.

These three stories indicate that Chandler was determined to make sham and facade his theme from the beginning. The superficiality extends from actors to gangsters and politicians, a tableau spanning American life. Unfortunately, the Prohibition era, so convivial to the theme, was over, though in blackmail and kidnapping Chandler found serviceable substitutes. Money was his universal motive. What he lacked was a knight to unmask sham and deal justice while protecting innocence. Mallory had an appearance, but no ethos, interests, or thoughts. In fact, in the first story he appeared most concerned with his pay, just like other *Black Mask* detectives.

"Killer in the Rain"

Chandler discovered the first-person point of view in his fourth story, "Killer in the Rain" (*Black Mask,* January 1935). By giving his narrator the freedom to describe what he saw, Chandler was able to avoid some of the stereotypes and conventions that plagued detective fiction. The narrator could also tell the reader something about his feelings, usually through simile and hyperbole, which Chandler found he liked.

This story became the basis of Chandler's first novel. Anton Dravec hires the nameless detective to free his daughter Carmen from porn dealer Harold Steiner. Everyone is in love with Carmen: chauffeur Carl Owen, a "guy named Joe Marty," even Dravec, who reveals that he adopted her. The detective finds a drugged Carmen posing nude before the camera of Steiner, who is dead. But his body and her negative disappear after the detective takes Carmen home. He discovers Joe Marty transferring Steiner's porn books to his apartment, then chauffeur Carl Owen turns up dead. The detective makes a deal with Marty for the negative, but Carmen shows up with a gun. Then Dravec breaks down the door. After Marty and Dravec kill each other, the detective destroys the negative.

Chandler cited "*Carmen* as Merimée wrote it," rather than Bizet's opera, as one of his favorite stories (*SL*, 203). Although Chandler's Carmen is a vulgar imitation of the original, she elicits the same jealousy and murder that doomed Merimée's hero, José Navarro. She refuses to marry Carl Owen after eloping with him, like her namesake preferring the pleasure of many lovers. Chandler retained the character of the original Carmen, but interpreted her independence as promiscuity; in the place of Merimée's narrator, who loves Carmen and hears of her death from Navarro, Chandler put his detective, who hears Carmen's story from Dravec (a lover) and is himself sexually attracted to her. The tensions that could be generated within a triangle were considerable, as Chandler knew by having won Cissy from Julian Pascal.

In this story Chandler also discovered weather and colors as symbolic motifs. He made it rain in sunny Los Angeles: "I stared at the window, watched the rain hit it, flatten out, and slide down in a thick wave, like melted gelatin. It was too early in the fall for that kind of rain."[2] This aspect of the ballyhooed California climate corresponds to Steiner's porn world, where the nether side of human desire reigns. Chandler also began to use colors in symbolic schemes from which he varied little for the rest of his career. Green is the color of lust, of sensuality; Carmen dresses in a green and white coat, and wears green jade earrings. Red is the color of action and confrontation, while shades of gray and white ("scraped bone" or "putty colored") describe morally empty characters. If blonde may be deemed a color, it becomes clear in this story that no blonde woman is to be trusted: this was already a convention of the genre, but Chandler applied it with a new brutality.

The sex and sadism, overt and implicit, of "Killer in the Rain," broke new ground. Under "Cap" Shaw's direction, *Black Mask* had kept its heroines chaste. It featured a married detective and a couple who worked as a team, but aside from a kiss upon rescue for the hero, most of the sex occurred offstage. Hammett changed that, and Chandler had sufficient technique to make the pulp story leer. He saw that, when the description of sex had gone as far as permitted, a symbolic representation of sex followed by a graphic depiction of death could provide a comparable sensation. Here his detective finds Carmen:

She was wearing a pair of long jade earrings, and apart from those she was stark naked.

I looked away from her to the other end of the room.

Steiner was on his back on the floor, just beyond the edge of the pink rug, and in front of a thing that looked like a small totem pole. It had a round open mouth in which the lens of a camera showed. The lens seemed to be aimed at the girl in the teakwood chair.

....

Steiner was wearing Chinese slippers with thick white felt soles. His legs were in black satin pajamas and the upper part of him in an embroidered Chinese coat. The front of it was mostly blood. His glass eye shone brightly and was the most lifelike thing about him. At a glance none of the three shots had missed. (*KR*, 8–9)

In this scene and another later the detective slaps women. The circumstances are carefully justified and the reader invited to enjoy the necessity of this misogyny. Carmen, for example, is drugged: "The tinny chuckling was still going on and a little froth was oozing down her chin. I slapped her face, not very hard. I didn't want to bring her out of whatever kind of trance she was in, into a screaming fit" (*KR*, 9).

Gas, Blood, and Guns

Three of the next four stories that Chandler wrote used rainy weather as a motif. "Nevada Gas" (*Black Mask,* June 1935) reverts to a third-person narrator and finds a new hero in tough-guy gambler Johnny De Ruse. He uncovers the murder/extortion plot of George Dial, his rival for Francine Ley. After killing his own boss, Dial has De Ruse kidnapped and taken for a ride in a cyanide gas car, from which De Ruse escapes. Patient legwork and information from gamblers Zapparty and Parisi lead De Ruse back to Dial, who dies when he attempts to run off with the wife of his dead boss.

The strong points of the story are the settings and the characterization of amoral types George Dial, Francine Ley, and De Ruse. The romance between Ley and De Ruse is one of the most complex male-female relationships that Chandler ever attempted, owing much to Hammett's portrayal of Nick and Nora Charles in *The Thin Man* (1935). The story introduces the gambling club, a setting that Chandler used increasingly, and employs abandoned stucco houses in the La Crescenta flood plain to amplify the rain motif wonderfully. But the story fails, despite the innovations, because of loose plot ends and the hero's lack of mythic resonance.

Chandler's plots often frayed at the ends because he was building scene by scene, refusing to discard good scenes that did not fit. Instead he adjusted the ending. The method he worked out was to abut dissimilar scenes, forcing the reader to absorb new characters and conflicts rather than permitting him to solve the story's "mystery." The source of this technique is revealed by a sentence describing the Club Egypt: "The balcony was high and the scene down below had a patterned look, like an overhead camera shot."[3] He discovered that narrative transitions could not only be left out, with the reader/viewer inferring them, but that this gave the story a sense of the texture of modern life. In a genre dominated by plot conventions, in which readers were accustomed to trying to guess what the author/hero would do next, Chandler became the most unpredictable, and thus interesting, by omitting transitions and simply abutting his best scenes.

When he began to write, Chandler admitted, he had read only one or two detective novels. His sixth story, "Spanish Blood" (*Black Mask*, November 1935), shows that he was studying the work of Dashiell Hammett. Chandler's hero shares the first name of Hammett's Sam Spade, and the story's depiction of big-city political bosses owes to Hammett's *The Glass Key* (1931). That novel's theme of a man's loyalty to his best friend in spite of their love for the same woman appealed to Chandler's sense that he had not wronged Julian Pascal. This story also pays tribute to Hammett's stoolies in Joey and Max Chill, to his drug addicts in Stella La Motte, and to his Filipinos in Cefarino Toribo. These were staples of Hammett's Op stories.

In spite of its debts "Spanish Blood" is exceptionally well done. It has a credible hero with a code and a past: Sam Delaguerra's *Californio* grandfather was one of the county's first sheriffs. "My blood is Spanish, pure Spanish. Not nigger-Mex and not Yaqui-Mex," Delaguerra tells a white politician. His name ("of the war") gives him mythic stature. When he is pulled off the murder of his longtime friend Donegan Marr ("We used to carry the torch for the same girl") by an Inspector who suspects his objectivity, Delaguerra investigates on his own, finding at Marr's cabin the body of the suspected assassin, Assistant District Attorney Imlay. Through stoolies and underworld contacts, Delaguerra learns that the political bosses, in league with Police Commissioner Drew, wanted Imlay off their election ticket. Only Delaguerra and Commissioner Drew survive the meeting in which the hero confronts the bosses with the truth. Drew proposes to credit himself with an undercover investigation that exposed the corruption. A realist, Delaguerra agrees. The story concludes with a twist when he visits Belle Marr and reveals that she, in fact, killed her husband. But since Marr covered up for her, intending that no one know, Sam says he will respect his friend's wish.

The story is well constructed and paced, the ending neither predictable nor overblown. The low-life characters are nearly as authentic as those of Hammett, but, what is more important, Chandler manages to make the desire for justice, which is the motive force, broad enough to accommodate both the idealism that drives Delaguerra to vindicate his dead friend and the cynicism of his realistic deal with Commissioner Drew.

The substance of "Spanish Blood" came from an actual incident that drew considerable press coverage. Charles Henry Crawford, the crime boss of Los Angeles, was gunned down 20 May 1931. Everyone's candidate for the rap was Guy McAfee, who had joined the L.A.P.D. after seeing a policeman roll a drunk and had risen through the vice squad to control Los Angeles casinos and gambling. But it turned out that the killer was an exceptionally good-looking Deputy District Attorney and candidate for judge known as Handsome Dave Clark.[4]

In "Guns at Cyrano's" (*Black Mask,* January 1936) Chandler continued his search for a persona and a hero. Told in the third person, this story introduces Ted Malvern (Ted Carmady in later editions.) He attempts to free blonde Jean Adrian and boxer Duke Targo from extortion by racketeers, but discovers that they in turn are blackmailing a local politician. The unexpectedly moral politician shoots the crime boss who uses him and then commits suicide. Since neither Targo nor Adrian garner any reader sympathy, the plot falls flat. In the resolution Chandler shot himself in the foot by explaining why one of the hirelings hadn't killed Jean in the opening scene.

Nevertheless, "Guns at Cyrano's" is an important story. Chandler worked hard to give his hero some humanity. Malvern pays attention to the lives of "little people," such as elevator operators, cigar-counter girls, and doormen. He gives the bellboys in his hotel five-dollar bills when they imply they're hungry. "Malvern the All-American sucker," he says of himself, "a guy that plays with the help and carries the torch for stray broads." As a hero Malvern fails because of such obvious pandering, and because Chandler makes him the scion of a fortune accumulated through political corruption. Saddled with wealth, Chandler's original sin, Malvern can't possibly become a democratic hero.

Chandler's mastery of repartee and ability to stretch the accepted generic limits of sex and violence had also advanced. Malvern's best lines are unpredictable. "I see our next trip is all arranged for," he says to his kidnapper when they pass a hearse (*PNS*, 137). As in "Killer in the Rain," Chandler finds new ways to substitute death for sex. When Malvern reports the bellboy's death to Jean, he uses its shock value as part of his seduction technique. "There's something horrible about you!" says Jean. "Something—satanic. You come here and tell me that another man has been killed—and then you kiss me. It isn't real." In a clever manipulation of archetypal plot situation and sexual nuance, Chandler has Malvern rephrase this charge: "There's something horrible about any man that goes suddenly gaga over another man's woman." When Jean exclaims "I'm not his woman," she justifies, in the masculine code, a seduction technique of kisses and death that even Chandler recognized as macabre.

The first seven stories have a similarity in plot deeper than their details. In his first story Chandler discovered the traitorous woman who causes her lovers' deaths in her quest for fame or money. He used variations on this type over and over, not because he was misogynic but because the type set up intense reactions among the men Chandler arrayed around her. He did not pretend to be able to write about women; men were the readers and principal characters of *Black Mask* stories. Once he discovered that this type solved all his plot problems, Chandler stuck with what worked, since by his own admission he was inept with narrative structure.

Resolving the relationship of the detective to the femme fatale was not as easy. Ideally the detective should have a love relation with her so that the reader felt the hero's life was threatened. In "Spanish Blood" and "Nevada Gas" Chandler made his detective the present or former lover of a woman who has been or may be won by another man. This detective, like Merimée's Navarro, is part of the triangle. But when Chandler allowed his detective to seduce the traitorous female in "Guns at Cyrano's" the triangle posed formula problems. Sentimental himself, Chandler couldn't end his detective's liaison in other than maudlin fashion.

Hammett did not offer Chandler any clues here. In "The Girl with the Silver Eyes" Hammett had sent Jean Delano (the model for Jean Adrian and "Silver Wig," Mona Mesarvey) to prison; at the end of *The Maltese Falcon* he sent Brigid O'Shaughnessy to probable death. But as Chandler's hero developed, sentimentality became his distinguishing feature; without it he had no special generic identity. The solution was to create a love triangle or circle (in the case of Carmen Dravec) in which one male was an analogue for the detective, who would be threatened symbolically. In "Killer in the Rain" Chandler hit on the first part of the solution with Carmen and her attraction to the detective, but not until "The Curtain" did he have his detective repeat the steps that led to Dud O'Mara's death at the hands of his stepson. These two subplots lay in loose relation until Chandler united them in *The Big Sleep*.

"The Man Who Liked Dogs"

Although the influence of Hammett reappears, Chandler soon passed from his sway to that of Ernest Hemingway, whose reliance on nouns and verbs, and short simple sentences connected by "and" are evident in "The Man Who Liked Dogs" (*Black Mask,* March 1936). Told in the first person, this story concerns detective Ted Carmady, whom the reader meets engaged in the humble work of checking veterinarians to find a dog: "There was a brand-new aluminum-grey De-Soto sedan in front of the door. I walked around that and went up three white steps, through a glass door and up three more carpeted steps. I rang a bell on the wall. Instantly a dozen dog voices began to shake the roof. While they bayed and howled and yapped I looked at a small alcove office with a rolltop desk and a waiting room with mission leather chairs and three diplomas on the wall, at a mission table scattered with copies of the *Dog Fancier's Gazette*" (*KR*, 46).

Carmady's code is an honest day's work for an honest dollar: when Chief Fulwider and Galbraith discuss the $1,000 reward on Farmer Saint, Carmady says, "You cut me out. . . . I'm on straight salary and expenses." Resistance to monetary corruption and sympathy for small people define Chandler's detective distinctly for the first time. He looks for a lost girl, Isobel Snare; bawls out Chief Fulwider ("You cleaned the town up once and you can do it again"); befriends ex-cop Red Norgard, and sympathizes with Diana and Jerry Saint.

Hemingway's code of courage is evident in the unreal amount of punishment that Carmady absorbs, though the way he shakes off the effects of morphine and alcohol still owes to Hammett (see "The Temple of the Holy Grail" in *The Dain Curse*). But dominating these influences is the sense of place and contemporary interest that Chandler imparts to this story. Not only is Bay City based on Santa Monica, but Chief Fulwider is a civic booster of the sort that dominated Los Angeles in the 1920s, much to Chandler's disgust: "Our little city is small, but very, very clean. I look out of my west window and I see the Pacific Ocean. Nothing cleaner than that. On the north Arguello Boulevard and the foothills. On the east the finest little business section you would want to see and beyond it a paradise of well-kept homes and gardens" (*KR*, 62). Other details, from the "disused interrurban right of way, beyond which stretched a waste of Japanese truck gardens" to the gambling ship *Montecito* and its water taxis, are authentic. Beginning with the *Johanna Smith* and *Monfalcone* in 1928, gambling ships operated beyond the two-mile territorial limit off Long Beach. Chandler was probably most impressed by the July 1935, storming of the *Monte Carlo,* when six men with automatic weapons seized the boat, chained the crew, and stole $35,000 in cash and jewels from passengers.[5]

So confident was Chandler in this story that he began to experiment with his tone. There are jokes in Spanish: the sanitarium where Carmady is drugged, imprisoned, and shot at is on Descanso ("rest") Street. There are topical references: the namesake of the gambling ship *Montecito* is a community north of Los Angeles with many millionaires. And there are multiple similes: "His eyes stuck out like peeled eggs. A thin trickle of saliva showed in the fat crease at the corner. He shut his mouth with all the deliberation of a steam shovel" (*KR*, 63). Chandler wrote later that "to break the mood of the scene with some completely irrelevant wisecrack without entirely losing the mood—these small things for me stand in lieu of accomplishment. My theory of fiction writing is that the objective method has hardly been scratched, that if you know how to use it you can tell more in a paragraph than the probing writers can tell in a chapter" (*SL*, 182).

For his first story outside *Black Mask* Chandler created another hero, perhaps wishing to keep Carmady within the pages of the magazine that nurtured him. Undercover vice-squad detective Peter Anglich appears only in "Noon Street Nemesis," later retitled "Pickup on Noon Street" (*Detective Fiction Weekly,* May 1936.) A less interesting hero, he seems to exist to let his author into the black flophouses and "cheat spots" of the Central District. These hovels are supposed to be as much part of the fabric of crime and fraudulence as Trimmer Waltz's Juggernaut Club and actor John Vidaury's Hollywood suite.

As in "Smart-Aleck Kill" and "Blackmailers Don't Shoot," the plot depicts the blackmail of a Hollywood figure by a racketeer. Again it turns out that the actor arranged the threats in order to revive his career. The subplot concerns Anglich's efforts to return a bedraggled girl named Token Ware to decent society. The sketches of the cook at the Bella Donna Diner, the clerk at the Surprise Hotel, and Rufe, Trimmer Waltz's bodyguard, were homework for Chandler's return to Central in "Try the Girl." The settings and social classes it surveys make this an interesting story, but the scenes are so disjunctive, united only by the denouement, that the reader struggles to make sense of them.

Carmady Returns

With "Goldfish" (*Black Mask,* June 1936) Chandler wrote the first of three stories in a row concerning Carmady, the detective of "The Man Who Liked Dogs." There are new elements: the story takes place in Olympia, Washington, and Westport, California, and the crime has already occurred. Wally Sype was caught stealing the famous Leander pearls and told his cellmate about the unrecovered loot. As the story is told, the cellmate is hiding because he knows too much, comforted only by the goldfish of the title, which becomes a symbol for humanity.

In "The Curtain" (*Black Mask,* September 1936) Chandler returned to the first-person point of view and his favorite plot. This time he set the love triangle of Larry Batzel and Dud O'Mara for Mona Mesarvey at one remove from Carmady, allowing him to avoid the sentimental excess that marred the end of "Nevada Gas." In the death of Batzel, which opens the story (repeating the male loyalty theme of "Spanish Blood") and his subsequent discovery that O'Mara is probably dead too, Carmady sees the fate that awaits him if he also succumbs to the temptations of "Silver Wig" Mona Mesarvey.

The hero of this story is basically the Marlowe of *The Big Sleep,* for which this story provided the basic plot. He is a working detective who calls on General Dade Winslow (the model for General Sternwood) and affirms the primacy of his code by turning down Winslow's offer of $1,000. He reveals his other important quality, sentimentality, when he takes the job of finding Dud O'Mara, whom he suspects is dead, though he does not want to tell the General. He likes the General, his pioneer heritage, and his love of O'Mara. Earlier, tougher versions of Chandler's private eye could have cared less. But Chandler, certain of his discovery now, made Marlowe quick to defend this feeling. When Lieutenant Roof snubs his effort to protect the General from news of O'Mara's death, Carmady responds "Maybe I'd go pretty far to attend to that sentiment" (*KR*, 119).

In spite of improbabilities such as Carmady shooting accurately with his hands cuffed behind him, this story ranks among Chandler's best efforts. The repartee is crisp and unpredictable. Like Francine Ley and Jean Adrian, Mona Mesarvey is a strong, independent woman able to match Carmady's wisecracks. It is important, in the convention of the "blonde" that Chandler exploited, for her platinum wig to fall off at the moment of truth, revealing her honest brunette heart. Chandler united his best motifs, from the rain to the oil boom, with a theme that he carried through the story from start to end: money corrupts. From the General's initial offer to the detective's discovery that Dade Winslow Trevillyan is "a little lad that likes money," Chandler pursues the sickness of wealth.

For "Try the Girl" (*Black Mask,* January 1937) Chandler added new facets to Carmady's character: a past on the police force and a dash of self-criticism. Cruising the Central district, he meets Steve Skalla, a white version of the giant Rufe. Skalla involves him in the death of the owner of Shamey's bar, where Skalla goes in search of his old flame Beulah. Skalla flees, but Carmady traces Beulah through interviews with decrepit Violet Shamey and Dave Martineau, studio manager at KLBL radio, where Beulah hosts the Jumbo Candy Bar program. Before he reaches Beulah, he accidentally tips Mrs. Martineau to her husband's infidelities: when Martineau turns up dead in Beulah's bed, Carmady suspects his wife, but Skalla arrives and says he committed the murder earlier. Mrs. Martineau shoots him, but when Beulah arrives Carmady finds that actually she killed Martineau. In a finale borrowed from "Spanish Blood," Carmady helps cover up Beulah's crime.

This story again stretched the generic conventions with regard to sex. To justify Beulah's claim of self-defense, Carmady beats her and tears her clothes to simulate an attack. "I hadn't even kissed her," he notes. "I could have done that at least. She wouldn't have minded any more than the rest of the knocking about I gave her." The sexual tension thus generated is dissipated with highly symbolic action, followed by death: "We rode the rest of the night, first in separate cars to hide hers in my garage, then in mine. We rode up the coast and had coffee and sandwiches in Malibu, then on up and over. . . . He died at two-thirty the same afternoon. She was holding one of his huge, limp fingers, but he didn't know her from the Queen of Siam" (*KR*, 168).

This is a more refined technique than he used in "Killer in the Rain," but Chandler shows in "Try the Girl" that he can manipulate these leers for humor too, as when he portrays Violet Shamey: "She got up out of the chair, sneezed, almost lost her bathrobe, slapped it back against her stomach and stared at me coldly. 'No peekin,' she said, and wagged a finger at me and went out of the room again, hitting the side of the door casement on her way" (*KR*, 138–39).

Such a scene is balanced by a new self-critical element in Carmady's character. After he gets Violet Shamey drunk to obtain information, he feels badly: "I was a nice boy, trying to get along. Yes, I was a swell guy. I liked knowing myself. I was the kind of guy who chiseled a sodden old wreck out of her life secrets to win a ten-dollar bet" (*KR*, 141).

Chandler was also finding new ways to avoid the chichés and stereotypes of the genre. From Hemingway he learned to understate the real emotion: "She began to laugh. Then she went over to the mirror and looked at herself. She began to cry" (*KR*, 168). His similes and hyperboles, though growing from the fad for "wisecracks," became ways to avoid clichéd descriptions. Chandler wrote that "except for the motor horns, the distant hum of traffic up on Sunset Boulevard wasn't unlike the drone of bees" (*KR*, 145). If he had written that the hum of traffic was like the drone of bees, readers would have yawned. By employing the cliché in a double negation, he ironically indicates both its utility and emptiness. The horns make the distant traffic *completely* unlike the drone of bees. Chandler's famous similes begin in this simultaneous dependence on and desire to burlesque conventional description: "The silence of that house was what made me go in. It was one of those utterly dead silences that come after an explosion. Or perhaps I hadn't eaten enough dinner. Anyway I went in" (*KR*, 153).

Once he began to mock the conventions, it was logical for Chandler to extend the burlesque by intruding on his narrator's thoughts. He tried it in the last scenes of "Try the Girl." Hearing Mrs. Marti-

neau's confession of how her husband's trysts led to her attempt to
kill him, Carmady remarks:

> "The story," I said: "I know how you felt. I've read it in the love mags
> myself."
> "Yes. Well, he said there was something about Miss Baring he had to see
> her about on account of the studio and it was nothing personal, never had
> been, never would be—"
> "My Gawd," I said, "I know that too. I know what he'd feed you. We've
> got a dead man lying around here. We've got to do something, even if he
> was just your husband." (KR, 157)

A writer who can move smoothly from such satire to the sentimental
conclusion of "Try the Girl" has clearly mastered the nuances of tone.

Chandler Leaves *Black Mask*

"Try the Girl" was Carmady's last appearance. Along with several
other writers, Chandler stopped submitting to *Black Mask* when its
new owners fired editor "Cap" Shaw. Chandler continued the character under the name of John Dalmas in *Dime Detective,* where he published "Mandarin's Jade" in November 1937. An excellent story,
which Chandler used in *Farewell, My Lovely,* this piece features an ex-
emplary cast of minor characters.

Lindley Paul hires Dalmas to help ransom a jade necklace, but Paul
is beaten to death by thugs. Dalmas meets Carol Pride, a police
chief's daughter turned journalist, whose contacts turn up most of his
leads. Her imperfections ("an upper lip a shade too long and a mouth
more than a shade too wide"), like those of Steve Skalla, mark her as
a serious character, unlike the standard types of the genre. Dalmas
tells her, "You've got the sweetest set of nerves I ever met on a
woman," and Chandler notes that she "held her light as steadily as
any tough old homicide veteran." Like most positive female characters
in Chandler, she holds her own in repartee; in several places she initi-
ates double entendres: "I saw your little light flickering around down
in the hollow and it seemed to me it was pretty cold for young love—
if they use lights." Chandler so enjoyed setting these two wits in opposition that he sometimes let Carol dominate an exchange. It provided him with an occasion for authorial intrusion, as when Carol

remarks: "Now you've got me doing the wisecracks" (*KR*, 185, 180, 179, 181, 187).

Equally memorable are such minor characters as Second Planting, a Hollywood Indian whom Chandler surely saw in the streets of Los Angeles when he arrived, and his boss, Soukesian The Psychic, who represents the cultism of Los Angeles. Soukesian's cult fills the function of fraudulence that Chandler usually assigned to Hollywood: "I had a rough idea of what his racket would be and what kind of people would be his customers. . . . He would be an expert in frustrated women, in tricky, tangled love affairs, in wandering boys who hadn't written home, in whether to sell the property now or hold it another year, in whether this part will hurt my type with my public or improve it" (*KR*, 188–89).

Chandler's detective is by this point such a flexible vehicle, ranging from tough to sentimental, that he can make witty observations on his own poverty: "I unlocked the communicating door, which looked better than just kicking the lock lightly—which had the same effect—and we went into the rest of the suite, which was a rust-red carpet with plenty of ink on it, five green filing cases, three of them full of California climate, an advertising calendar showing the Dionne quintuplets rolling around on a sky-blue floor, a few near walnut chairs, and the usual desk with the usual heel marks on it and the usual squeaky swivel chair behind it" (*KR*, 185).

The plot of "Mandarin's Jade," when unraveled, is a variation on the love triangle. Mrs. Prendergast has been playing her two lovers, Soukesian and Paul, against each other to get her necklace back. If one or both were killed, that simply eliminated blackmail. She seeks to draw Dalmas into the same pattern, asking him to investigate a bar near the Hotel Tremaine; when he does, he's sapped and nearly killed except for Carol's intervention. The teetotaling Carol stands as a dramatic foil to the drunken Mrs. Prendergast, giving a greater variety of female characters and more complexity of plot than Chandler had previously managed with the triangle.

"Red Wind" (*Dime Detective,* January 1938) is a lesser effort, despite its reputation. Having had success with unseasonable rain as a setting, Chandler set this story during the rasping hot Santa Ana winds of May, thought to promote irritability and crime. As in the previous story, the story centers on a stolen necklace and blackmail. Chandler acknowledges his source in an authorial intrusion: "I suppose you've read that story. About the wife and the real pearls and her telling her husband they were false?" "I've read it . . . Maugham," says Dalmas, alluding to Somerset Maugham's story "Mr. Know-all."[6]

In the story Dalmas witnesses a murder in a bar, then in his apartment house runs into a woman described by the victim. Lola Barsaly wanted to buy back her pearls from the dead man because they were a present from an old love. Dalmas's work on her behalf leads him to confront tough cops Copernik and Ybarra and eventually to her husband, whom Dalmas finds with his mistress. The dead man had been blackmailing both Barsalys. Dalmas sets everything straight with everybody; he even has a cheap set of pearls made for Lola, hiding the fact that the originals, as in Maugham, were quality imitations. Such excess sentiment, present throughout, torpedoes the tale.

Chandler set aside Dalmas to try a different kind of detective in "The King in Yellow" (*Dime Detective,* March 1938). The hero is smoother and the plot capitalizes on contemporary interests. Hotel detective Steve Grayce loses his job when he throws out a famous jazz trombonist named King Leopardi, so he becomes a private detective. When the musician turns up dead in the bed of old girlfriend Dolores Chiozza, Grayce takes on the task of clearing her. It turns out that the murder avenges the suicide of a girl mistreated by Leopardi years earlier. Her brothers planned to kill him in the room where their sister died, but Grayce unwittingly interfered, so they killed him at Chiozza's apartment. In the resolution one brother kills the other, and Grayce allows the survivor to escape in return for a signed confession. The survivor commits suicide by running his car off the mountain highway, a finale Chandler reused in *The Lady in the Lake.*

While a competent piece of craftsmanship, "The King in Yellow" does little more than demonstrate Chandler's knowledge of music and tour the Bunker Hill shabbiness that he had already described so well. The plot has the usual holes: Why did the brothers send Leopardi a ransom note asking for $10,000? What is Jumbo Walters's function in the story? The story does not represent any advance in technique or theme.

With "Bay City Blues" (*Dime Detective,* June 1938) Chandler returned to Dalmas and a first-person narrator. This story had so much action and so many interesting characters that it begged to be developed; it became Chandler's fourth novel, *The Lady in the Lake.* The story grew from a new plot idea, the murder of one woman by another who is a vicious bitch with a history of using and discarding men. Dr. Leland Austrian's wife is murdered by his nurse Helen Matson, a "red-haired man-eater with no looks but a lot of outside curves." When Dalmas meets Matson she is at a gambling club, trying to blackmail the owner because Mrs. Austrian was his mistress and died after leaving his club. Helen is independent, audacious, and imperfect, like Chandler's positive female characters. But she is a redhead and the convention for the type prevails. She has already dumped Harry Matson, the colleague who ensnared Dalmas in the case, as well as Al De Spain, a demoted Bay City homicide detective modeled on Galbraith in "The Man Who Liked Dogs."

De Spain is a brutal sadist, whose beating of "Big Chin" Lorenz is often cited by critics as the most violent scene in Chandler's work. He cannot adequately be explained as an expansion of the genre's limits on violence. Despite Chandler's efforts to justify the scene through Dalmas's protest that "I felt sick at my stomach," most readers finish the two pages of close detail feeling they have witnessed something very foul. De Spain also commits the brutal execution and simulated rape of Helen, his old flame, for which he frames Dalmas. Incredibly, at the story's end Dalmas says, "The hell of it is I liked De Spain. He had all the guts they ever made." Insofar as the story justifies De Spain, it puts Chandler uncomfortably close to Mickey Spillane, whom he professed to detest. The designation of De Spain as the villain in *The Lady in the Lake* suggests that Chandler realized his error in the short story.

Minor characters are developed in more detail than usual in Chandler's stories. Dr. Austrian turns out to have complex reasons for covering up his wife's murder; he shares the propensity of Donegan Marr ("Spanish Blood") and Steve Skalla ("Try the Girl") for protecting guilty lovers. Newsman Dolly Kincaid is a nice thumbnail portrait, as is De Spain's sidekick Shorty. Portrayed for the first time is Los Angeles homicide detective Violets McGee, a frequent source of cases for Chandler's detectives, so named because of his fondness for violet-scented breath mints.

Chandler set several of his stories at Big Bear Lake in the San Bernardino Mountains, a summer retreat that he and Cissy enjoyed. It appears in scenes of "Spanish Blood" and "The King in Yellow." With "The Lady in the Lake" (*Dime Detective,* January 1939) he set most of a story in the mountains. That the lake invigorated him is shown by the crisp, detailed descriptions of the scenery and the crowds of tourists: "Hundred-foot yellow pines probed at the clear blue sky. In the open spaces grew bright green manzanita and what was left of the wild irises and white and purple lupine and bugle flowers and desert paintbrush. The road dropped to the lake level and I began to pass flocks of camps and flocks of girls in shorts on bicycles, on motor scooters, walking all over the highway, or just sitting under trees showing off their legs. I saw enough beef on the hoof to stock a cattle ranch" (KR, 303).

Chandler also enjoyed creating Deputy Sheriff Tinchfield, who is an expansion of house detective Kuvalich in "Nevada Gas." In contrast to his urban representatives of law Chandler made Tinchfield the apotheosis of justice and diligence. Chandler's ear for accents and colloquialisms played with the opportunities Tinchfield afforded. "You wait here, son. I'll be back in a frog squawk," he says, and later "Where at are you stayin', son?" (KR, 312, 321).

In plot, however, "The Lady in the Lake" repeats "Bay City Blues." A vicious redhead kills another woman and gets two men, Howard Melton and Bill Haines, to be her saps. Like De Spain, Melton seems to square with Dalmas, but he too has killed his wife. This similarity permitted Chandler to unite the plots in The Lady in the Lake. There are new motifs, cosmetics and doubling, but they are not much exploited. Howard Melton is a cosmetics executive, and Beryl Haines has hair "a dark red color with glints of blue in the shadows— dyed" (KR, 329). She applies her rouge roughly, leaving prominent red blotches, and a guest at Goodwin's house uses a lipstick called "Carmen." Julia Melton and Beryl Haines look like sisters and are similarly promiscuous; Dalmas is not sure which is which in photos at first. But Chandler did not follow up the possibilities of these motifs.

Planning Greater Things

As this succession of stories suggests, Chandler was enjoying a period of quality production. He began to plan The Big Sleep in 1938, and in March 1939 wrote out a schedule for other books. "Since all plans are foolish," he wrote, "let us make a plan." He described what became Farewell, My Lovely, The High Window, and a third novel never written. These were to support him as he wrote a "short, swift, tense, gorgeously written" drama called "English Summer" and "a set of six or seven fantastic stories," among which he listed "The Bronze Door" and "The Disappearing Duke." The novels were to "make enough money for me to move to England and to forget mystery writing," he wrote. As he embarked on this plan, Chandler cleared his desk of manuscripts and in new stories ventured from his usual material.[7]

"Pearls are a Nuisance" (*Dime Detective,* April 1939) is one of his strangest and funniest stories. On the one hand, it is a satire in which Chandler pits the English and American mystery schools against each other and lampoons the conventions of all detective fiction. On the other hand, as several critics have noted, its scenes are blatantly homoerotic.

The story is told by a first-person narrator, Walter Gage, who speaks the King's English: "I cannot seem to change my speech. . . . my father and mother were both severe purists in the New England tradition, and the vernacular has never come naturally to my lips, even while I was in college" (*SAM,* 191). Pushed by his prim fiancée Ellen Macintosh, Gage tries to recover a dowager's fake pearl necklace (a satire on "Mandarin's Jade" and "Red Wind"). This leads him to her recently departed chauffeur, Henry Eichelberger. The two fight, drink, argue, wake up in the same bed, and decide to cooperate in solving the case; they are Natty Bumppo and Chingachgook, Huck and Jim, in the storied land of male camaraderie. It turns out that the pearls are real, given by an admirer who could afford them but didn't want the dowager to worry (a twist on Maugham's "Mr. Know-all.") The admirer ransoms them, and the heroes engage in a round of carousing. At last the apparently naive Gage turns up Henry, who had the pearls all along.

Through the interleaving of formal and vernacular speech Chandler makes several technical points about dialogue. On the whole it is a successful piece of humor, the only pure comedy among Chandler's stories, but it has provided fuel for critics, such as Gershon Legman, who argue that "Chandler's Marlowe is clearly homosexual—a butterfly, as the Chinese say, dreaming that he is a man."[8]

Less interesting is the widely anthologized "Trouble is My Business" (*Dime Detective,* August 1939), told by John Dalmas in the first person. He is hired by Anna Halsey for a difficult case involving heir Gerald Jeeter and his lover Harriet Huntress, a friend of gangster Marty Estel. Jeeter's father wants Huntress to vanish. Dalmas investigates and finds that the previous detective on the case died; then he's held up by two thugs, one of whom takes a shot at him and is later killed by the Jeeters' chauffeur. Dalmas is warned off the case by gangster Estel, but solves it when he finds Gerald dead in Harriet's closet, killed by the chauffeur. It's an unsatisfying plot and hardly anything in Chandler's repertoire of wisecracks, femmes fatales, or brutality seems to click. It has a weariness that suggests he just wanted it off his desk.

Chandler finally succumbed to the "slicks" when he wrote "I'll Be Waiting" (*Saturday Evening Post*, 14 October 1939). The plot is a mishmash of earlier stories. Hotel detective Tony Resick is a tubby Steve Grayce ("The King in Yellow"). He finds Eve Cressy (Eve Millar) listening to Benny Goodman in the lobby (where Grayce listened to Leopardi). She's waiting for her ex-husband, whom she "put in a bad place" (like Beulah in "Try the Girl"). Tony's hoodlum brother arrives and tells Tony that the "trouble boys" are waiting for her ex-husband because he welshed on a gambling scheme. But he is already in the next room, unknown to Eve, so Tony sneaks him out without Eve learning that he came. Later he hears that both his brother and her ex-husband are dead and returns to Eve, one of Chandler's tough/tender women, to revel in his bittersweet knowledge. Like "The King in Yellow," this story has informed appreciations of jazz and classical music. It was a powerful, successful piece for the *Post*, yet Chandler disliked it: "It was too studied, too careful. I just don't take to that sort of writing. The story was all right, but I could have written it much better in my own way, without trying to be smooth and polished, because that is not my talent. I'm an improviser, and perhaps at times an innovator" (*SL*, 434).

Chandler wrote two more short stories about his detective, but only one is of consequence. "No Crime in the Mountains" (*Detective Story*, September 1941) uses the Big Bear Lake setting of "The Lady in the Lake" and was incorporated into the novel. The portrait of Sheriff Baron repeats that of Tinchfield, and his assistant Andy is a development of Tinchfield's helper Paul Loomis. Detective John Evans, telling the story in the first person, is called to Puma Lake to see Fred Lacey, only to find him dead. An Oriental named Charlie saps Evans and spirits away his body. The rest of the plot explains how the five hundred real dollars that Lacey stuffed in the toe of his wife's shoe turned into five hundred counterfeit dollars. The answer is that the Japanese Charlie and Nazi Frank Leuders are counterfeiting U.S. currency to weaken the economy. The plot is so bad that one critic suggests Leuders should have shot the narrator instead of himself. There are a few good scenes in the resort town of Indian Head, but the story is most notable for its World War II hysteria.

The other short detective story was written in the late fifties, when Chandler had lost his powers but Philip Marlowe was a known name. It has several titles: "Marlowe Takes on the Syndicate," "Wrong Pigeon," "Philip Marlowe's Last Case," and most commonly "The Pencil." It is an awful pastiche of dated tough-guy dialogue, modern revelations about the Cosa Nostra, and predictable plotting. Chandler fans should avoid it.

Fantastic Stories

As his work plans reveal, "the fantastic genre" tempted Chandler in the late 1930s when he was bored by the detective story. Although he was highly critical of science fiction, he was fascinated by the idea of characters who could disappear. "The Bronze Door" (*Unknown,* November 1939) and "Professor Bingo's Snuff" (*Park East,* June/August 1951) combine this mildly supernatural motif with mystery plots. The second, more interesting story concerns a man who kills his boarder, after the latter sleeps with the man's wife and strangles her. He doesn't care about his wife; he simply takes advantage of the invisibility afforded by Professor Bingo's Snuff to carry out his fantasies. His tendency to make himself invisible in bathrooms and to meet strong men strengthens the Legman school of analysis.

There is also an unfinished Marlowe story titled "The Poodle Springs Story," which details the married life of Marlowe and Linda Loring after *Playback.* They move to a thinly disguised version of Palm Springs, trade backchat, and become parodies of themselves: "I browsed on her eyebrows and her lashes, which were long and tickly," says Marlowe. He runs into gangster Manny Lipshultz, but the manuscript ends just when the reader has reason to hope that Lipshultz will bump off this travesty of the once-noble Marlowe.[9]

English Summer

"English Summer: A Gothic Romance" is a longish story that Chandler mentioned in his writing plan of 1939, but did not finish until the mid-fifties. First-person narrator John Paringdon tells the story, set in the English country cottage of Edward Crandell. The visiting narrator had a longstanding, unreciprocated crush on Millicent, Crandell's wife, so every encounter is pregnant with a Jamesian delicacy of meaning and unexpressed emotion. They joke mildly about her swaggering husband; the narrator apologizes for his American expressions and habits. Indeed, he sounds a bit like Marlowe.

Down at the lake, the narrator meets Lady Lakenham, a temptress on a black stallion whose sexual significance is obvious to everyone but the author. The first chapter ends on their kiss. Almost immediately they arrive at her shambling estate; the exterior is woolly with vines, the interior ravaged. The second section ends with the pair in bed.

When he returns, Millicent asks Paringdon if he ever has loved her. He says yes, and on his way upstairs decides he must leave. Coming back down, he announces his decision and they have tea. Millicent says Edward is drunk; he had a quarrel with Lady Lakenham, and she lashed him with her crop and ran him down with her stallion. Paringdon realizes he is in the middle of a triangle, but when he goes to get his bag, he finds Crandell dead.

Here the plot line breaks. Paringdon becomes a detective; his first thought is to save Millicent by framing Edward. But she responds that she killed him because he was being "cheap" and "a little more brutal than usual." Paringdon engineers a suicide scene and departs, intending never to see Millicent again.

For three weeks he hides, but a constable and a Scotland Yard man catch up with him. It's clear from their questions they know what happened. Paringdon sees Millicent at the inquest, but doesn't speak to her. Later he meets Lady Lakenham by Green Park in Piccadilly; she's still a man-eater and wants him to come see her in her rooms the next day. He agrees, knowing that he is leaving before then. The story ends: "I stood there for what seemed a long, long time, looking after nothing. There was nothing to look after."

The story shares many features of *The Long Goodbye,* such as the taking of tea with the murderess, and it would be interesting to know if these were in the 1939 sketch or added later. While intriguing, the story is seriously flawed by the break in tone and Chandler's inability to control the sexual motif. Unfortunately, this was as close as he came to his dream of escaping the detective genre.

Chapter Five
High Spirits
The Big Sleep

Many readers consider Chandler's first novel, *The Big Sleep* (1939), to be his best, and even dissenters rank it second or third. It was written in a burst of three months when Chandler was fifty, the plot provided by his short stories. The writing is fresh and polished, almost in a new voice.

Philip Marlowe, making his debut, goes to the Sternwood mansion to see the ailing patriarch of an oil fortune. The entry-hall, dominated by ancient decor and funereal silences, contains a stained-glass mural of a knight rescuing a naked maiden tied to a tree. As he waits, Marlowe meets Carmen, one of two daughters causing the old man problems. One of Chandler's blondes, she is a nymphomaniac with deformities that type her as a succubus. From the outset the tone established is what Edward Margolies calls "Los Angeles gothic."

Marlowe meets General Sternwood, who seems "to exist largely on heat, like a newborn spider," in a humid greenhouse filled with orchids. He tells Marlowe that he just gave Joe Brody $5,000 to disappear from Carmen's life, and now Arthur Gwynn Geiger has sent him gambling IOUs signed by Carmen: Marlowe's job is to remove these "morbid growths." He also mentions that his son-in-law, former Irish freedom fighter Rusty Regan, has vanished and that Marlowe resembles him. "The private, soldierly virtues" of Sternwood, which are the only moral virtues in the novel, notes Margolies, "are about to die with him," appreciated only by Marlowe and Regan.[1]

On his way out Marlowe meets the other daughter, lusty Vivian (Rusty's wife), who questions him. Then he goes off to read up on rare books since Geiger is a bookseller. At Geiger's shop he questions a blonde clerk, Agnes Lozelle, who can't answer his bibliographic queries, then he tails a customer and confirms his suspicion that Geiger rents out pornography.

He waits in the rain and follows Geiger home, then hears shots

from the house. Breaking in, he finds Carmen naked and Geiger dead
on the floor before a camera. Carmen is drugged; Marlowe slaps her
around and gets her dressed. Searching the house, he finds Geiger's
client list but no photo plates. He drops Carmen at the Sternwood
mansion and walks back, but Geiger's body has vanished.

The next morning Bernie Ohls of the District Attorney's office invites Marlowe to the Lido pier to see the body of Owen Taylor, a
Sternwood chauffeur who once eloped with Carmen. Taylor appears to
have been sapped before his car ran off the pier, but his death is never
cleared up. Years later when Howard Hawks filmed the novel, he
telegraphed Chandler "Who killed Owen Taylor?" "I don't know,"
Chandler replied.

Back at Geiger's shop, Marlowe sees books being loaded on a
truck. He traces them to the apartment of Joe Brody, then returns to
his office, where Vivian Regan is waiting. She shows him a print of
Carmen naked and a blackmail note. She proposes to get the hush
money from gambler Eddie Mars, at whose roulette tables she is a
regular; besides, she says, Mars's wife ran away with her husband.

Marlowe finds Carmen trying to recover the negatives at the scene
of Geiger's still-undiscovered murder. He slaps her around again, but
as they are leaving Eddie Mars arrives and questions Marlowe. Then
Marlowe calls on Joe Brody and Agnes, who hold him at gunpoint.
Carmen appears, this time armed, but Marlowe manages to take all
the guns and send her home. Brody admits to the blackmail, but is
killed when he answers the door. Marlowe gives chase and captures
Geiger's lover Carol Lundgren, modeled on Wilmer in *The Maltese
Falcon*. Back at Geiger's house, Marlowe finally finds the body and
calls Detective Ohls. The police grill him for not reporting the murder, but he acquits himself.

On the third morning Marlowe interviews Captain Gregory of
Missing Persons about Rusty Regan. His car was found in Mona
Mars's garage, says Gregory, who doesn't really want to discuss Regan. Marlowe gets suspicious. The Sternwood butler calls to give
Marlowe the General's thanks; a check for $500 is in the mail. But
Marlowe decides to pursue the unassigned job of finding Regan. He
visits Eddie Mars's club and learns that Gregory is under Mars's
thumb. Then he watches Vivian win $32,000 at the roulette table
and, after rescuing her from one of Mars's men, takes her for a drink
and liaison in lover's lane, where he pumps her for information. She
is insulted.

At his apartment, Marlowe finds Carmen in his bed. She won't get out, despite threats, until he says he'll throw her in the hall naked. After she curses him and leaves, he tears his bed apart in frustration.

On the fourth morning Marlowe confronts Harry Jones, Agnes's latest beau, who offers him the location of Mona Mars for $200. Marlowe buys, but when he arrives at the rendezvous Lash Canino, Mars's gunman, is squeezing Jones for information and then kills him with arsenic-laced whiskey. Agnes, however, has the address and, when she phones in, Marlowe arranges to meet her. Mona Mars is in a house behind a garage in the desert near Realito.

On his way to Realito Marlowe gets a flat tire by the garage: "Fate stage-managed the whole thing," writes Chandler. Inside the garage, Canino and a mechanic get the drop on Marlowe and sap him. When he wakes, he is at the feet of Mona Mars, who is impressed by his bluster and cuts him loose (save handcuffs). Groggy and half in love, he kisses "Silver Wig" and begs her to come with him, but she loves Eddie Mars. Marlowe runs to his car, gets a gun, and with Mona's aid, shoots Canino when he returns: he is the only man Marlowe ever kills.

On the fifth day Marlowe and the police settle accounts; then he goes to see the General, who upbraids him for pursuing Regan. When Marlowe offers to refund his money, the General offers him $1,000 more to find Regan. On his way out Marlowe meets Carmen and returns her handgun. She says she wants to learn to shoot and drives him to a deserted oil rig where she has practiced before. When she fires five blanks at Marlowe, the cause of Regan's disappearance becomes clear.

Marlowe confronts Vivian with the facts: Carmen killed Regan because he refused, as Marlowe did, to sleep with her. Vivian panicked and called Eddie Mars, who dumped the body in an oil sump, and sent his wife to the country to make it appear that Regan had run off. Then Mars set Geiger on the General to see if he knew of the murder and was ripe for blackmail. At the novel's end Marlowe broods on death ("the big sleep") and Mona, the woman who helped him escape it.

An Unnecessary Journey

The theme rises from what Dennis Porter has called "the ironic form of an unnecessary journey."[2] Marlowe is searching for a man the

General and his butler say Marlowe resembles. The search leads him unwittingly through scenes in Regan's life: friendship with the General, attraction to and conflict with Vivian, rejection of Carmen, and infatuation with Mona Mars. They have the same relationships to these characters, but Marlowe reads Regan's life as a morality play detailing the dangers of wealth and dissipation. A second parallel for Marlowe is sentimental little Harry Jones, who follows Geiger and Brody as the third sap in the life of Agnes Lozelle, for whom he dies. From these two examples, and the plot's revelations about its female characters, Marlowe learns that he caught the culprit in the opening scene, when Carmen fainted into his arms. The novel is, as one critic put it, an "anti-romance." At its end, all four women survive, but of the five men involved with them only Marlowe remains alive, contemplating "the big sleep" to which they have sent the others.

Structure and Sources

Chandler built *The Big Sleep* out of four short stories that he had written in the previous five years. As Philip Durham notes in his introduction to *Killer in the Rain*, Chandler combined plots and characters from "Killer in the Rain," and "The Curtain" with bits of "Mandarin's Jade" and "Finger Man":

To illustrate Chandler's method of combining and enlarging plots, one can see in *The Big Sleep*, for example, how the author drew from "The Curtain" for Chapters 1–3, 20, 27–32 and from "Killer in the Rain" for Chapters 4, 6–10, 12–16. With the exception of small bits borrowed from "Mandarin's Jade" and "Finger Man," Chapters 5, 11, 17–19, 21–26 were added. Ten chapters were drawn from "The Curtain," eleven were taken from "Killer in the Rain," and eleven were almost all new material. The twenty-one borrowed chapters, however, were expanded beyond their original state in the short stories. (*KR*, ix)

In essence, what Chandler did was take the tone—from the omnipresent rains to the prurient interest—of "Killer in the Rain," which featured attractive, demented Carmen Dravec and pornographer Steiner. This he laid over the stronger plot line and supporting characters of "The Curtain," which featured a murderous child, the ailing General, and a blonde named Mona.

The record of Chandler's progress may be read in the chapters that he added and rewrote. The first new material (chap. 5) is ordinary, but chapter 11 (chap. 6 of "Mandarin's Jade"), concerning Vivian Regan's visit to Marlowe's office, is made more credible by the reduced emphasis on drinking. Vivian is not only more believable than Mrs. Prendergast of the short story, but new sexual repartee heightens the tension between her and Marlowe. In chapter 17 Chandler changed the culprit from Carmen's father to a slick homosexual whose motive is revenge for the murder of his lover, a change that makes the plot line more confusing but aligns the sexual motifs better.

New chapters 18 and 19 provide a reasonable accounting by Marlowe to the police. They serve as the denouement of the first two murders and build a bridge to the second story that is completed when one of Eddie Mars's thugs waits for Marlowe as he returns from Taggert Wilde's house. As transitional chapters that patch together disparate stories, these are not bad: one can see much cruder work in Hammett's first novel, *Red Harvest*.

In chapters 24–29, reworking the sensational cyanide death car material of "The Curtain," Chandler began to hit his stride, and the reader can watch a novelist discovering his powers. The pace of the chapters not only improves, but Chandler clarifies the allegoric importance of Carmen when she appears in his bed, repeats metaphors in patterns (the knight on the chessboard, Harry Jones as a bird, Canino as a motor), and emphasizes Marlowe's classic detective code. In five pages Chandler discovers:

—how to justify the finely honed tropes he made small-time hoodlums speak: "The little man wasn't so dumb after all. A three for a quarter drifter wouldn't even think such thoughts, much less know how to express them."[3]

—how to excuse his own plots: "I . . . sat in my chair thinking about Harry Jones and his story. It seemed a little too pat. It had the austere simplicity of fiction rather than the tangled woof of fact" (*BS*, 158).

—how to make setting contribute to theme: "I turned into the narrow lobby of the Fulwider Building. A single drop light burned far back, beyond an open, once gilt elevator. There was a tarnished and well-missed spittoon on a gnawed rubber mat. A case of false teeth hung on the mustard-colored wall like a fuse box in a screen porch. I shook the rain off my hat and looked at the building directory beside the case of teeth. Numbers with names and numbers without names. Plenty of vacancies or plenty of tenants who wished to remain anonymous. Painless dentists, shyster detective agencies, small sick businesses that had crawled there to die, mail order schools that would teach you how to become a railroad clerk or a radio technician or a screen writer—if the postal inspectors didn't catch up with them first. A nasty building. A building in which the smell of stale cigar butts would be the cleanest odor" (*BS*, 159).

Despite these discoveries, and its striking triumphs, *The Big Sleep* is flawed in several important ways. It is two stories, patched together. There is no logical necessity in Marlowe's continuing, against the General's directions, to discover the fate of Rusty Regan in the second half of the novel. Indeed, the discovery that Carmen is a murderess in the last pages raises a question: how could she earlier have missed Joe Brody at such close range?

Chandler got away with the plot because he was a superb scenarist. Individual scenes are so well written, so engaging, that the reader is overwhelmed by what Edgar Allan Poe said was of primary importance: "the construction of the effect." Chandler bears him out. He articulates a world bewilderingly filled with detail and incident, the nature of which, as revealed by simile, hyperbole, and irony, seems to be godless, a world of matter and laws of physics. But the tropes and the repartee work from an assumption that somewhere, somebody has things figured out. It is, of course, the author or his proxy, the detective. A worldview is implicit in the metaphors, which constantly make connections between people, events, items, and feelings, hinting at some coherence. They prepare the reader to accept the unity of understanding offered by the detective code, which is the oversoul of the various tropes.

Chandler's Universe of Metaphor

Chandler's most noticeable stylistic trait is his use of metaphor. While previous detective novelists made use of it to clarify physical situations or to sketch quickly their myriad minor characters, Chandler created a world in which metaphor was as important as characterization or plot.

In Chandler's work there are two principal types of metaphor. The first is oral: the wisecrack or repartee. It occurs in conversations, is ironic, and serves the "tough guy" atmosphere. It is discussed in chapter 6. The second kind of metaphor is thought by Marlowe in order to help the reader apprehend the situation. These metaphors are more elaborate, even fantastic, and point to an alternate construction of reality. As Poe's Dupin said in "The Purloined Letter," "The material world abounds with very strict analogies to the immaterial."

An example of this second use is the variety of metaphors by which Marlowe portrays Carmen Sternwood in the first four pages:

> walked as if she were floating
>
> teeth . . . as shiny as porcelain
>
> lowered her lashes like . . . a theatre curtain
>
> sucked her thumb . . . like a baby with a comforter
>
> went up the stairs like a deer (*BS*, 2–4.)

These tell the reader that she is not only young and agile, but also infantile and mentally defective: "artificial" is the concept that Chandler seems to have had in mind. Carmen is a kind of puppet: ". . . as if [she had] artificial lips and had to be manipulated with springs" (*BS*, 147).

In Marlowe's first encounter with Vivian Regan metaphors give her a lusty sex appeal: "the ankles long and slim and with enough melodic line for a tone poem." But after this, to a striking degree, she becomes the metaphoric match of her sister. Her teeth "glittered like knives." Her room is "artificial as a wooden leg," and like Carmen she seems a marionette: "her hand went up slowly like an artificial hand worked by wires" (*BS*, 14, 130, 207, 212).

Several times Chandler reuses an elaborate metaphor that he has associated with a character in order to foreshadow a repetition of an appearance or situation. This happens twice with Carmen, whose giggles are like rats running behind the wainscoting of an old house; with Harry Jones, compared several times to birds; and with Lash Canino, who has "a purring voice, like a small dynamo behind a wall." When Canino toasts Harry Jones with a glass of cyanide, Marlowe guesses what is happening because "the purring voice had an edge, like sand in the bearing" (*BS*, 172, 161).

This last motif illustrates the prevailing tendency of Chandler's metaphors; they posit a mechanistic, post-Einsteinian world, a world of time, space, mass, motion, and inertia. Chandler's comparisons are constantly to size, speed, impact, balance—the physical relations of matter. The General "nodded, as if his neck was afraid of the weight of his head." Geiger "will think a bridge fell on him." Norris has "a back as straight as an ironing board." Agnes's "smile was hanging by its teeth and eyebrows and wondering what it would hit when it dropped." An "army of sluggish minutes dragged by" Marlowe. Agnes put her face "together again, as if lifting a great weight" and "chipped at the air with one hand." Eddie Mars's hair is "as fine as if it had been sifted through gauze." Brody has "hair like steel wool" and changes his voice, when dealing with Marlowe, from a "ten ton truck" to "a scooter." Newspaper stories are as close to the truth "as Mars is to Saturn." Eddie Mars's casino is decorated in "elaborate patterns, with the accuracy of a transit." A minute sound is "like a small icicle breaking." Marlowe's "brain ticked like a clock." Unconscious, his mind is a "darkness in which something red wriggled like a germ under a microscope." Somebody, he says on waking, "built a filling station on my jaw" (BS, 7, 12, 13, 20, 29, 47, 79, 62, 70, 80, 110, 127, 160, 193, 177, 178).

A second motif on which Chandler relied for metaphor was California life. Marlowe's world abounds in comparisons to the common objects of daily life in Los Angeles. The General saves his strength "as carefully as an out-of-work showgirl uses her last good pair of stockings." The coastline has "a loud sea-smell which one night's rain hadn't even dented." Marlowe's cabinets are full of California climate. The muzzle of Eddie Mars's Luger looks "like the mouth of the Second Street tunnel," but at least he hasn't made his casino "look like an MGM set." And there are the orchards: Carmen has teeth as white as orange pith, the "flawless lines of the orange trees wheeling away like endless spokes" as Marlowe drives, Vivian has "eyes as large as mammoth prunes" and Carol Lundgren has "moist dark eyes shaped like almonds" (BS, 6, 41, 51, 67, 121, 3, 170, 51, 90).

More surprising, however, is the domestic realm to which Chandler goes for many metaphors. A great number of comparisons have to do with animals: dogs, cats, birds, and horses. Marlowe remarks that Carmen's coyness is "supposed to make me roll over on my back with all four paws in the air." The General sniffs at Marlowe's cigarette "like a terrier at a rathole." Vivian chews her lip "like a puppy at the fringe of a rug." Marlowe tells Carmen, who is crawling after her gun, "You look like a Pekinese." The dog's life is clearly not the detective's; he compares himself to a cat at least twice: "Our eyes were like the eyes of two tomcats on a wall." "I walked like a cat on a mantel" (BS, 3, 7, 17, 81, 133, 161).

Things that Chandler noticed around the kitchen also create a sense of familiarity about what is really a frighteningly physical universe.

A greenhouse of orchids is like a "slow oven," and Marlowe is "trussed like a turkey, ready for the oven." Someone's face "falls apart like a bride's pie crust," while another is "as hard and white as cold mutton fat." "You're no English muffin, yourself lady," says Marlowe, later noting that someone "would hardly weigh as much as a butcher's thumb." Mona is "slim but not a dried out crust," while Canino looks at Marlowe "as if he was looking at a slab of cold meat." Chandler's world overflows with these household sights; he has metaphors on furniture, on renting an apartment, and on drinking tea; but the kitchen seems to have been his favorite domain (*BS*, 5, 178, 47, 97, 139, 151, 179, 174).

Opposed to this domestic world is one of metaphoric disease and death. From the first pages, in which the General's orchids are described as "plants with nasty meaty fingers and stalks like the newly washed fingers of dead men," to the last, in which the General's "thoughts were as grey as ashes," the novel is poxy with death. The General has "eyes from which all fire had died long ago," the "outward turning earlobes of approaching dissolution," and "licks his lips like an undertaker dry-washing his hands." He "looked a lot more like a dead man than most dead men look" and tells Marlowe that his job is "removing morbid growths from people's backs." Agnes is "as sore as an alderman with mumps." "Dead men are heavier than broken hearts" and Harry Jones has "the sort of smile the operating room sees." There's a "huge canopied bed, like the one Henry the Eighth died in." And finally, there is Rusty Regan's death: "You were dead, you were sleeping the big sleep" (*BS*, 5–7, 201, 12, 37, 152, 196, 215).

Philip Marlowe, Knight

Marlowe sketches himself for the reader in his interview with General Sternwood: "I'm thirty-three years old, went to college once and can still speak English if there's any demand for it. There isn't much in my trade. I worked for Mr. Wilde, the District Attorney, as an investigator once. His chief investigator, a man named Bernie Ohls, called me and told me you wanted to see me. I'm unmarried because I don't like policemen's wives." He adds that "I was fired. For insubordination. I test very high on insubordination" (*BS*, 7–8).

This insubordination, blended with Marlowe's irony, becomes an attractive quality for a mass readership that works in offices and on assembly lines, and rebels against the faceless nature of life. When the General says he too is insubordinate, the reader perceives the quality to animate the independent, the entrepreneurs. To be insubordinate or ironic is to join an elite, to be a risk-taker. This assumption by the reader of insubordination and irony is satisfying and inexpensive.

Other passages reveal that Marlowe drives a convertible, make unknown, in which there is a secret compartment for a gun and frequently a bottle of rye. A citizen of Los Angeles, he lives in an apartment building called the Hobart Arms, which has a plate-glass door, an elevator, and a bare, square lobby with a potted palm. His apartment is an efficiency, for he mentions a kitchenette and he finds Carmen in his Murphy bed. Despite the scant space, Marlowe has a sense of place: " . . . this was the room I had to live in. It was all I had in the way of a home. In it was everything that was mine, that had any association for me, any past, anything that took the place of a family. Not much; a few books, pictures, radio, chessmen, old letters, stuff like that" (BS, 107–8, 143, 147).

Waiting for him on his chessboard when he comes home is a knight's problem. The image of the "knight" is Marlowe's cross and hairshirt. The knight is the historic antecedent of the detective, but Marlowe's irony would suggest that his code is hopelessly anachronistic in the modern world. The reference to the knight in the stained-glass window at the beginning of the book is followed by this one when Marlowe finds Carmen in his bed: "I went over . . . to the chessboard on a card table under the lamp. There was a problem laid out on the board, a six-mover. I couldn't solve it, like a lot of my problems. I reached down and moved a knight, then pulled my hat and coat off and threw them somewhere. All this time the soft giggling went on from the bed, that sound that made me think of rats behind the wainscoting in an old house." A page later, failing to solve the woman in his bed, Marlowe notes, "I looked down at the chessboard. The move with the knight was wrong. I put it back where I had moved it from. Knights had no meaning in this game. It wasn't a game for knights." The motif is carefully balanced by a third reference just before Marlowe's last interview with the General: "the knight in the stained-glass window still wasn't getting anywhere untying the naked damsel from the tree." Ironic as he may be, Marlowe is no less than a knight: it is his awareness of his code that nourishes this irony (BS, 144, 146, 195).

Marlowe has an office, location uncertain in this novel, but memorably described: "a room and a half on the seventh floor at the back. The half-room was an office split in two to make reception rooms. Mine has my name on it and nothing else, and that only on the reception room. I always left this unlocked, in case I had a client, and the client cared to sit down and wait." In his reception area are a "faded red settee, the two odd semi-easy chairs, the net curtains that needed laundering and the boy's size library table with the venerable magazines on it to give the place a professional touch (*BS*, 50–51). In the office proper are the famous five green filing cases of California climate so well described in the short stories.

Marlowe's Code

In this novel Marlowe embraces the traditional detective code, ignoring liberalizations introduced by Hammett and Gardner. Chandler makes its chivalric origins clear on page one:

Over the entrance doors, which would have let in a troop of Indian elephants, there was a broad stained-glass panel showing a knight in dark armor rescuing a lady who was tied to a tree and didn't have any clothes on but some very long and convenient hair. The knight had pushed the vizor of his helmet back to be sociable, and he was fiddling with the knots on the ropes that tied the lady to the tree and not getting anywhere. I stood there and thought that if I lived in the house, I would sooner or later have to climb up there and help him. He didn't seem to be really trying." (*BS*, 1)

This passage sets up the figure of the detective/knight, his problem with naked and/or amorous daughters to whom he must be sociable, and the solution: a pragmatist stepping into the idealized tableau to achieve results. The chivalric figure fiddles with knots; the modern detective unties people, or, as Chandler ironically reversed the situation, the maid (Mona) unties the knight (Marlowe).

Marlowe's code is also revealed by his reactions to the lascivious Sternwood daughters. Finding the naked Carmen in Geiger's house, Marlowe says, "I looked her over without either embarrassment or ruttishness. As a naked girl she was not there in that room at all. She was just a dope. To me she was always just a dope" (*BS*, 32). Several uncomprehending critics have scored Marlowe's "rejection, for no discernible reason, of the blandishments of the Sternwood daughters."[4]

But a review of the original scene in "Killer in the Rain" shows that it was rewritten to emphasize resistance to lust. This is a tenet of the early Marlowe's detective code.

This feature develops, albeit with prurient overtures to the audience, as Marlowe dresses Carmen, and when he later throws her out of his bed. Even when he necks with Vivian, his intent is to elicit information: "What has Eddie Mars got on you?" he keeps asking as they embrace. When Vivian jokes that men have been shot for questions like that, Marlowe replies, "Men have been shot for practically nothing. The first time we met I told you I was a detective. Get it through your lovely head. I work at it, lady. I don't play at it" (BS, 141).

Resistance to sexual temptation originates in the chivalric tradition of courtly love, in which the chaste virgin is worshipped from afar by the anguished poet. In its tough update, however, the pining detective sometimes releases his frustration on homosexuals and deviants. In *The Big Sleep* the most unpleasant villain, Carol Lundgren, is a homosexual with a bisexual first name. While Gershon Legman's complaint that "Mr. Chandler seems to be sold on the proposition that homosexuals have the pornography business tied up" seems to be based on a misreading of the plot, there is a high level of homophobia:[5]

> ". . . had a stealthy nastiness, like a fag party."
>
> ". . . like Caesar, a husband to women and a wife to men."
>
> ". . . Joe Brody didn't kill your queen." (BS, 58, 92, 91)

But Marlowe does not sympathize with heterosexual voyeurs either. He describes the pornography buyer he tails as a "woodpecker" whose head wobbles as he walks. "People who spend their money for second hand sex jags are as nervous as dowagers who can't find the rest room," says Marlowe. As for promiscuity, Carmen is a warning. Marlowe has more respect for sentimental little Harry Jones and his devotion to Agnes. All these motifs unite to emphasize the novel's traditional sexual outlook (BS, 75).

Respect for the law is a second important feature of the early Marlowe's code. Ironic as he is, Marlowe believes that the bad guys are bad and the police, flawed as they may be, are better. When Vivian says that "all a police record means in this rotten crime-ridden country" is not knowing the right people, Marlowe says, "I wouldn't go that far." When Mona Mars asserts that "As long as people gamble there will be places for them to gamble," Marlowe lectures her: "That's just protective thinking. Once outside the law you're all the way outside. You think [Mars] is just a gambler. I think he's a pornographer, a blackmailer, a hot car broker, a killer by remote control, and a suborner of crooked cops. He's whatever looks good to him, whatever has the cabbage pinned to it. Don't try to sell me on any high-souled racketeers. They don't come in that pattern" (*BS*, 52, 181).

Willful waffling between right and wrong annoys Marlowe. There is no middle ground for him, as there was for Hammett's Continental Op; the police the Op met were allied with or worse than criminals. *The Big Sleep* contains a corrupt police captain, but important figures like Ohls and D. A. Wilde are unimpeachable. Nor does Marlowe find the characters of the underworld useful: he does not employ informers or fraternize with bootleggers. He is aware of his legal powers—a result of the growing popularity of the police procedural novel—and his accountability to the rules is stressed by his interrogation in the district attorney's office at the denouement of each murder.

Honesty in financial dealings is the third outstanding feature of Marlowe's code. When Vivian asks if he is really so scrupulous, he replies, "Painfully." His standard charges are $25 a day and expenses; for the solution of the blackmail case he merits "fifty dollars and a little gasoline." He turns down a proffered payoff from Mars: "Information was the way I understood it," he says. When the General accuses him of betraying his trust in pursuing Regan's disappearance, Marlowe responds:

"I'd like to offer you your money back. It may mean nothing to you. It might mean something to me."
"What does it mean to you?"
"It means I refused payment for an unsatisfactory job. That's all." (*BS*, 52, 123, 197)

All three times that Marlowe explains how the detective code dictates his conduct, he emphasizes his proletarian demeanor. "I'm on a case," he tells the district attorney. "I'm selling what I have to sell to make a living. What little guts and intelligence the Lord gave me and a willingness to get pushed around in order to protect a client" (*BS*, 106).

Talking with the General about his unauthorized pursuit of Regan, Marlowe is more didactic: "When you hire a boy in my line of work, it isn't like hiring a window-washer . . . and saying: 'Wash those and you're through.' *You* don't know what I have to go through or over or under to do your job for you. I do it my way. I do my best to protect you and I may break a few rules, but I break them in your favor. The client comes first, unless he's crooked. Even then all I do is hand the job back to him and keep my mouth shut" (*BS*, 199).

Marlowe's ultimate expression of his code comes when Vivian Regan, at the novel's end, calls him a son of a bitch for exposing Carmen as Rusty's killer and offers him a $5,000 bribe. "Uh-huh. I'm a very smart guy. I haven't a feeling or a scruple in the world. All I have the itch for is money. I am so money greedy that for twenty-five bucks a day and expenses, mostly gasoline and whiskey, I do my thinking myself, what there is of it; I risk my whole future, the hatred of the cops and of Eddie Mars and his pals, I dodge bullets and eat saps, and say thank you very much, if you have any more trouble, I hope you'll think of me" (*BS*, 213).

The Women in Marlowe's Life

Vivian Regan is modeled on Vivian, the mistress of Merlin the Enchanter in *Le Morte D'Arthur*. She is beautiful, black-haired, intriguing, but like her namesake a liar, withholding from Marlowe (formerly Mallory) the key piece of information and spying on him to determine his mandate from the General.

It often seems that Marlowe has a genuine interest in Vivian. His banter grows progressively less hostile and more provocative. They share a drink in his office, after which, displaying the photo of Carmen's body, Vivian ventures, "You ought to see mine." "Can it be arranged?" asks Marlowe coolly. But his attention is a tactic: the detective code places the daughters of the client off limits. Vivian values appearances above truth and serves finally as a symbol of duplicity. She lives in a sham world of the rich. And the rich, says Marlowe, make him sick (*BS*, 56, 59).

Carmen Sternwood unites two stereotypes, or conventions, of popular fiction. One is the blonde, a favorite sexual provocateur of American melodrama, the other the succubus, an archetype that dates to the Middle Ages. Used most adroitly in the American detective novel by Hammett, the succubus is marked by a physical deformity and limited mentality. Carmen is blonde, has "little sharp predatory teeth" and "a curiously shaped thumb, thin and narrow like an extra finger, with no curve in the first joint." The ravages of drink and drugs have left her a human husk: "I could see, even on short acquaintance, that thinking was always going to be a bother to her." Like the succubae of medieval lore, she appears in the hero's bed unexpectedly at night: "Carmen Sternwood lay on her back, in my bed, giggling at me. The tawny wave of her hair was spread out on the pillow as if by a careful and artificial hand. Her slaty eyes peered at me and had the effect, as usual, of peering from behind a barrel. She smiled. Her small sharp teeth glinted." To sleep with a succubus is to risk losing one's soul. Marlowe avoids this fate; however, not sleeping with the succubus turns out to be equally dangerous. She kills Rusty Regan for rejecting her advances and attempts to kill Marlowe for the same reason (*BS*, 3, 143–44).

The woman who interests Marlowe is Mona Mars, whom he nicknames "Silver Wig." Marlowe has only secondhand information on the former Mona Grant, a cabaret singer, until late in the novel. After he is sapped and tied up, he wakes at her feet: "She was so platinumed that her hair shone like a silver fruit bowl. She wore a green knitted dress with a broad white collar turned over it." Green is the color of desire in Chandler, and Mona's platinum hair, in accord with the convention about blondes, turns out to be a wig. She yanks it off after Marlowe's speech about "protective thinking": beneath is short-cropped hair, which was dark in "The Curtain" (*BS*, 178).

To the reader it is unclear whether his grogginess or his enchantment with Mona accounts for Marlowe's subsequent giddiness. She gives him a drink and, after some banter, cuts him loose. When they embrace, Marlowe says "Her face under my mouth was like ice." This coldness has led to speculation: some critics feel it shows Marlowe's homosexuality, others that it shows Mona is an illusion, the coldness signifying her unreality. "I never saw her again," Marlowe notes. It is also possible that Chandler was practicing Hemingway's art of "objective realism," revealing an emotional state through physical details. Mona's coldness would indicate that she is extremely frightened by her situation; for the same reason her hands shake and her laughter is "racking" (*BS*, 185). A thorough reading of all Chandler's novels will show that Mona is in fact the girl with the "cornflower blue eyes," unattainable because she belongs to Chandler's early period of innocence.

Critical Reception

Looking back after twenty years, notes Philip Durham, "it is difficult to imagine why reviewers, even then, decided that *The Big Sleep*
was so completely hard-boiled." But they did: The *New Yorker* called
it a "terrifying story of degeneracy in Southern California by an author who almost makes Dashiell Hammett seem as innocuous as
'Winnie-the-Pooh.' " *Time* reported that "Marlowe is plunged into a
mess of murderers, thugs and psychopaths who make the characters
of . . . James Cain look like something out of *Godey's Lady's Book*."[6]
   The Big Sleep has become a classic. Detective-novel fans ranked it
third in a recent poll asking them to name the best mystery stories
of all time. The scholars are equally unanimous. The counterpoint of
detail and discovery led Dennis Porter to rate it equal or over *The
Hound of the Baskervilles* and *The Moonstone*. Peter Rabinowitz terms it
an "extraordinary novel," Dilys Powell calls it "the best of the Chandler books," and Peter Wolfe says "the book deserves its place as a
classic of the hardboiled literary detection."[7]

Farewell, My Lovely

Chandler's second novel is unique among twentieth-century American novels, a feast of similes, an ark of grotesques. The "fast episodic
manner of *The Big Sleep*," writes Gavin Lambert, gives way to "a jig-
saw structure, equally rapid and complex, but firmer."[8]
   Foremost among the grotesques is garishly dressed Moose Malloy,
a lovelorn giant whom Marlowe meets outside Florian's, the Negro
bar where Moose seeks his old flame Velma. When a Negro bouncer
tries to throw him out, Malloy maims him and kills the bar's owner.
Marlowe is a witness to the crime.
   Goldbricking, racist Lieutenant Nulty gets the case and persuades
Marlowe to investigate. Marlowe urges Nulty to look for Velma.
From the clerk at the hotel across from Florian's he learns that Florian's widow is alive. When he plies the alcoholic Mrs. Florian with
bourbon, he finds that she has an old photo of and some connection
to Velma. He reports his discoveries and self-disgust to Nulty.
   A second plot line begins when Lindsay Marriott calls with a job:
Marlowe is to pay an $8,000 ransom for a jade necklace. The pair
drive to a remote site, but no one is around. When Marlowe goes to
look, he is sapped and wakes up talking to himself, only to meet

spunky Anne Riordan, freelance journalist and "the kind of girl Marlowe would have married had he been the marrying kind."[9] Having found Marriott's body, she holds Marlowe at gunpoint until he dissuades her. They search the body, finding and withholding marijuana "jujus," then Marlowe reports to the police. This time Lieutenant Randall, the foil to Nulty, questions him. After he tells nearly all, Randall warns him off the case. In the first of several comic false alarms Nulty says the police have arrested Malloy.

In his office the second day Marlowe finds Anne waiting. She has discovered that Mrs. Lewin Lockridge Grayle owned the jade necklace and persuaded her to hire Marlowe. The plots of the two original stories link when it is revealed that Mr. Grayle owns KFDK radio, for Velma was a singer.

Dissecting the "jujus," Marlowe finds the cards of psychic Jules Amthor and arranges an appointment. Then he learns that Marriott held a lien on Mrs. Florian's house and interviews a neighbor, Mrs. Morrison, who reveals that Mrs. Florian gets a registered letter each month. Marlowe revisits Mrs. Florian, revealing what he knows about Marriott, but she won't talk.

Anne introduces Marlowe to the Grayles at their mansion, then she and Mr. Grayle leave. Marlowe and Helen Grayle drink and neck until Mr. Grayle returns. Then Helen invites him to meet her at Laird Brunette's gambling club that night.

Second Planting, a Hollywood Indian, is waiting in Marlowe's office. He produces Amthor's card and a $100 bill, then drives Marlowe to Amthor's hilltop aerie. There's a strained conversation, then the room goes black. Second Planting holds Marlowe, Amthor pistol-whips him, and two policemen, whom Marlowe calls Hemingway and Mister Blane, give him "the ritual beating that private detectives must take before they are allowed to carry on." Chandler tries to use the occasion to parody Hemingway, but falls flat.[10]

Marlowe wakes up in a private hospital suffering delirium tremens. He overpowers the attendant and escapes, glimpsing Malloy on the way out. The director says an Officer Galbraith committed him. Fortunately Anne Riordan's house is close; she feeds and repairs him and asks him to spend the night, but he returns to his apartment.

When he wakes on the third day, Lieutenant Randall is at his door with questions about Malloy and Marriott: Anne has revealed the withheld evidence. Marlowe and Randall retrieve the marijuana and visit Mrs. Florian, whom they find dead. Back at headquarters, in a celebrated scene, Marlowe devotes his attention to a pink bug rather than to Randall's theories about the murders.

Next Marlowe complains to Chief Wax in corrupt Bay City about Galbraith and Blane; he calls in Galbraith and says that Marlowe wants to visit Amthor again; instead they have a talk. Galbraith tells Marlowe that he can find Malloy through Laird Brunette, on the gambling ships offshore.

At nightfall Marlowe leaves his Venice Beach hotel, taking a water taxi to the *Montecito*, but is turned back for carrying a gun. Gentle giant (and putative homosexual) Red Norgaard puts Marlowe aboard commando-style for $25. On the boat deck Marlowe pulls his gun on Laird Brunette. Once Marlowe figures out who he is, they effect an exchange: Marlowe tells how he got aboard and Brunette agrees to pass a message to Malloy.

Back on shore Marlowe calls Mrs. Grayle about their date, and she agrees to come over. Marlowe takes a nap, waking to find Malloy, whom he hides in the closet when Mrs. Grayle knocks. Then Marlowe reveals her as Velma: she turned in Malloy, killed Marriott, and intended to kill Marlowe. When Malloy erupts from the closet, she shoots him five times. He dies that night.

Among the loose ends cleared up by Marlowe and Anne Riordan over drinks are several improbabilities: the photo of Velma wasn't Velma after all; Jesse Florian gave Marlowe's card to Marriott. Nor does the case conclude neatly: Mr. Grayle is in love with Velma and won't cooperate. To spare him pain, Velma commits suicide after shooting a policeman who recognized her in a Baltimore nightclub. "Casting Velma as a deliberate martyr who dies to save her husband's dignity," Liahna Babener explains, is "a more palatable rendition" of the grim truth that she is an inveterate trickster and killer.[11]

Like Othello, to whom Marlowe alludes in the final lines, Malloy "loved not wisely, but too well." He would have Velma as his Desdemona, except that romantic love is a relic: "Modern outspokenness has utterly destroyed the romantic dream on which love feeds," wrote Chandler. "There is nothing left to write about but death, and the detective story is a tragedy with a happy ending." Velma is an example of a West Coast phenomenon identified by Paul Skenazy: "The California Myth grants magical, transformative power to alterations of place, and to the impulses of individual will: 'out of sight, out of mind.' . . . Little Velma, a two-bit singer and moll, becomes Mrs. Lewin Lockridge Grayle, a woman of fashion."[12] Marlowe, who necks with Velma, who spies on Malloy and brings him face to face with her infidelity, is cast in the role of Iago, hence his constant discomfort. But the theme of impossible love applies to him as well, for he rejects Anne Riordan.

Technique in *Farewell, My Lovely*

Like Chandler's first novel, *Farewell, My Lovely* has its origin in short stories. The Velma Valento plot comes from "Try the Girl," while the portrait of corrupt Bay City, Dr. Sonderborg, and the gambling ships appeared first in "The Man Who Liked Dogs." Jules Amthor and his Indian helper, as well as the theft of the jade necklace, were central elements in "Mandarin's Jade." The recycled plots mesh better than they did in *The Big Sleep* because Chandler united the female characters of the first two stories and dropped the gunplay in favor of personal confrontations between Marlowe and his antagonists. On the other hand, the plot lacks necessity in many places. Psychic Jules Amthor and his Indian medium are given the barest rationalization in the denouement; otherwise they, and Dr. Sonderborg's private hospital, have little connection. Much of the material from "The Man Who Liked Dogs," such as Marlowe's trip to the *Montecito*, is similarly tangential. Marlowe's explanation of why Marriott is killed but he is not ("because it's bad business killing a man who is sort of a cop") is feeble at best. Chandler continued to be a scenarist.[13]

But he made several technical advances. He found leitmotifs that filled the potholes in the plot and reinforced the detective code. The contrast between the lazy, racist, publicity-hungry Lieutenant Nulty and clever, theorizing Lieutenant Randall provides humor and emphasizes the value of work, a subtheme. The investigation of the first murder goes nowhere because Nulty is inert: "Nulty didn't seem to have moved. He sat in his chair in the same attitude of sour patience. But there were two more cigar stubs in his ashtray and the floor was a little thicker in burnt matches" (*FML*, 29).

In his phone calls Nulty claims to have Moose Malloy cornered, only to announce later that he had the wrong car or arrested the wrong man. Finally he drops the case. The efficient Lieutenant Randall characterizes Nulty in a hyperbole more typical of Marlowe: "up near Crestline there's a place where a bunch of old box cars have been made into cabins. I have a cabin up there myself, but not a box car.

These box cars were brought up on trucks, believe it or not, and there they stand without any wheels. Now Nulty is the kind of guy who would make a swell brakeman on one of those box cars" (*FML*, 170). While Nulty provides comic relief between the murders of the novel's first half, Randall provides the energy needed to resolve them and close the case in the second half.

The greatest technical advance in *Farewell, My Lovely* is in Chandler's presentation of Marlowe's consciousness. Several times the reader enters Marlowe's mind as he makes a discovery, is sapped, or as he wakes. On these occasions the stream-of-consciousness technique includes the reader in the process of discovery. But it slows the narrative, and when a character is as metaphoric, ironic, and hyperbolic as Marlowe, the shift must be deftly managed.

In Chandler's first exercise with this technique he uses the frame of a conversation: Marlowe has been sapped, wakes up and converses, reconstructing the event, with another voice.

"Yeah, that was about how it was," the voice said.
It was my voice. I was talking to myself, coming out of it. I was trying to figure the thing out subconsciously.
"Shut up, you dimwit," I said, and stopped talking to myself. (*FML*, 53)

This is crude, but on the next page Chandler does better, burlesquing Hemingway's style and managing a pun on pulp magazines: "I felt the back of my head. My hat was still on. I took it off, not without discomfort and felt the head underneath. Good old head, I'd had it a long time. It was a little soft now, a little pulpy, and more than a little tender. But a pretty light sapping at that. The hat had helped. I could still use the head. I could use it another year anyway" (*FML*, 54).

By the middle of the novel Chandler had perfected the technique and could use it as he pleased, even for a transition between Mrs. Florian's house and Nulty's office: "I went in through the swing doors and found a uniformed lieutenant behind the railing looking over the charge sheet. I asked him if Nulty was upstairs. He said he thought he was, was I a friend of his. I said yes. He said okey, go on up, so I went up the worn stairs and along the corridor and knocked at the door. The voice yelled and I went in." (*FML*, 98–99)

The Growth of Marlowe

There are a number of new details about Marlowe in *Farewell*. His office is in the Cahuenga Building, Room 615, on Hollywood Blvd. near Ivar. The building is fictitious, but the location is just west of the present Hollywood Freeway, below the Hollywood Bowl. The office is above a coffee shop, next to offices that produce a constant clatter of typewriters.

Marlowe lives a half mile east, at the intersection of Franklin and Kenmore, below Griffith Park. He has acquired a pipe, which he smokes at home in preference to his work-day Camels. He thinks it gives him an air of solidity. He is six feet tall, weighs 190 pounds, and is "good-looking" if we trust Velma. He likes cats, drinks bourbon from pint bottles, carries a pencil flashlight in his pocket, and prefers the .38 revolver.

As in *The Big Sleep* he sketches himself and his trade in an interview with his client. But the exposition he gives Mrs. Grayle is shorter than that he gave General Sternwood: "There's not much money in it. There's a lot of grief. But there's a lot of fun too. And there's always a chance of a big case. . . . Most of us are ex-cops. I worked for the D. A. for a while. I got fired" (*FML*, 106).

As he develops, Marlowe's amazing store of technical knowledge and his use of literary metaphor pose a growing problem in consistency of characterization. He simply knows too much for a detective. In *The Big Sleep* Chandler tried to excuse his arcane knowledge: he has a college degree. But he does not prepare the reader in *Farewell, My Lovely*, and the abuses of consistent characterization are glaring. Marlowe discourses on or refers to the Dalai Lama, St. Swithin's Day, Electra complexes, chenille, point lace, pewter, Roman senators, Hessian leather, griffins, gimbals, arabesques, gems, French drip coffee, Richelieu, frozen capital, Pierrot girls, and Cremona violins.

A Humane Detective Code

One of the great attractions of Chandler is the way his detective's code evolves from novel to novel. The morality of *Farewell, My Lovely* begins where that of *The Big Sleep* concluded: Marlowe trusted Vivian's promise to seek help for Carmen, partially because he recognized his own complicity in the world's hypocrisy: "Me, I was part of the nastiness now" (*BS*, 216). This was a humane interpretation of the code's application, but Chandler furthered it in *Farewell* by putting his detective's fears, doubts, and mendacities in the foreground of the reader's attention, veiling the code itself until the time came to decide right from wrong.

The chief signal of his growing humanity is Marlowe's capacity for self-criticism. Chandler embellished the reaction that Marlowe had to Violet Shamey ("Try the Girl") in his interview with Jesse Florian: "A lovely old woman. I liked being with her. I liked getting her drunk for my own sordid purposes. I was a swell guy. I enjoyed being me. You find almost anything under your hand in my business, but I was beginning to be a little sick at my stomach" (*FML*, 26).

When Mr. Grayle interrupts Marlowe's necking session with Mrs. Grayle, Chandler introduces a moral sensibility new to Marlowe's thinking: "I was holding her and didn't have a chance to let go. I lifted my face and looked at him. I felt as cold as Finnegan's feet, the day they buried him." Mrs. Grayle could care less, but Marlowe notes, "I felt nasty, as if I had picked a poor man's pocket" (*FML*, 113–14).

The most delightful device in the series of self-evaluations is the use of the Rembrandt calendar in Marlowe's office:

They had Rembrandt on the calendar that year, a rather smeary self-portrait due to imperfectly registered color plate. It showed him holding a smeared palette with a dirty thumb and wearing a tam-o'-shanter which wasn't any too clean either. His other hand held a brush poised in the air, as if he might be going to do a little work after a while, if somebody made a down payment. His face was aging, saggy, full of the disgust of life and the thickening effects of liquor. But it had a hard cheerfulness that I liked, and the eyes were as bright as drops of dew. (*FML*, 33)

Less frequent are the long proclamations of the code that interrupted *The Big Sleep*. Instead Chandler locates Marlowe in the difficulties of the reader's life: "I needed a drink, I needed a lot of life insurance, I needed a vacation, I needed a home in the country. What I had was a coat, a hat and a gun. I put them on and went out of the room" (*FML*, 202).

As in the preceding novel, Chandler defines his detective within and against the genre, which plays an active role in the imaginations of the characters and metaphors of the author. Lieutenant Randall examines Marlowe "corpuscle by corpuscle, like Sherlock Holmes with his magnifying glass or Thorndyke with his pocket lens" and talks "like a polite FBI man in a movie." Anne Riordan envisions Marlowe with a "charming light smile and a phony English accent like Philo Vance" (*FML*, 166, 242).

Marlowe and Work

Many scholars believe that the persistent appeal of the detective novel in America is somehow due to an embrace of the national ideology. Showing this in novels such as *Red Harvest* and *Farewell, My Lovely* is difficult because they portray corrupt political systems. But national myths are also imbedded in attitudes, commonplaces, and figures of speech. Chandler's attitude toward work in this Depression-era novel reveals far more about his popular appeal than his comments on Los Angeles politics, about which he knew little.

He put Marlowe in the economic shoes of his readers and made him cherish the struggle for survival. When Marlowe gets sapped he feels badly, but "not as sick as I would feel if I had a salaried job." Though they contrast for humorous purposes, Nulty and Randall are public servants who emphasize Marlowe's independence. "Twenty million dollars wouldn't scare you," Marlowe tells Randall. "But you might get orders." When Nulty says he needs a break, Marlowe answers ironically "A man who works as hard as you do deserves one." Both the self-reliance and antigovernment attitudes expressed here are popular forms of a prevalent Social Darwinism (*FML*, 162, 163, 100).

In the national myth, wealth is open to the charge that it was gained without work; that was the rumor about Jay Gatsby. Lindsay Marriott's house is a place "where anything could happen except work." Jules Amthor patronizes women "with one thing in common—money." Anne Riordan's modest wealth is carefully justified. The worthless Marina del Rey lots sold to her honest, hard-working father by a chiseler produce an oil bonanza. People who wear expensive clothes, such as John Wax, are usually crooked: Lieutenant Randall has to explain that his suit cost $27.50 to allay Marlowe's suspicion (*FML*, 40, 87, 165).

In contrast, Marlowe observes a Franklinian parsimony. When Anne complains that Marlowe has no one to answer his phone, he says "I save money." He tells Mrs. Grayle "I'm a poor man, but I pay my

own way. And it's not quite as soft a way as you would like." When
Red Norgaard refuses extra money from Marlowe, he immediately
joins this round table of parsimonious knights (*FML*, 74, 190, 219).

Grotesques

Chandler peopled *The Big Sleep* with conventional criminals, small
and big-time, exaggerated but recognizable. For *Farewell, My Lovely*
he assembled a cast of lonely giants, drunken widows, Hollywood Indians, indolent policemen, traveling psychics, and sphinxlike hotel
clerks. They are walking similes, Dickensian dreams.

The popularity of grotesques in American fiction is thought to
grow out of national interest in the literature of the frontier. Tall
tales and frontier sagas were rich in characters whose peculiar physical
attributes were outward signs of their interior natures. Humorists
such as Bret Harte and Mark Twain employed these types liberally,
but it was Sherwood Anderson, in the stories of *Winesburg, Ohio*, who
humanized these characters to the point that readers recognized themselves in grotesques. Subsequently a number of Southern writers,
William Faulkner and Flannery O'Connor among them, used grotesques in their fiction.

One reason *Farewell, My Lovely* is so different from *The Big Sleep* is
that the characters with whom Marlowe deals have this wistfulness,
this American loneliness that gnaws at them. We often forget that
the novel opens with Marlowe searching for a barber who has run
away from his wife: "she was willing to spend a little money to have
him come home" (*FML*, 1).

Once extricated from the metaphors describing him, Moose Malloy
is the grotesque of romance, like "a hunky immigrant catching his
first sight of the Statue of Liberty." His eyes "had a shine close to
tears that grey eyes often have." Like Wing Biddlebaum, one of Sherwood Anderson's grotesques, he is characterized by his hands: "a hand
I could have sat in," "wrecking my shoulder with his hand," a hand
"into which his whiskey glass melted almost out of sight," "looked
like a toy pistol in his hand." When Velma shoots him, "the bullets
made no more sound than a hand going into a glove" (*FML*, 1, 2,
3, 7, 9, 240).

He hasn't seen Velma in eight years, she hasn't written to him in
six, and yet he believes. He loves her. "We was to of been married,"
he says, "when they hung the frame on me." He sets the novel in

motion, then disappears for most of two hundred pages, until Marlowe wakes to find Malloy beside him: "his deep-set eyes were still somehow gentle." All is excused Malloy "because the big sap loved her—and still does. That's what makes it funny, tragic-funny." That he has been betrayed by romantic love does not dawn on Malloy until he steps out of the closet into Velma's presence. "Get away from me, you son of a bitch," she says (*FML*, 8, 233, 239, 240).

Jesse Florian is a less appealing but more finely drawn grotesque. Marlowe, who compares himself to Rembrandt, paints her portrait in his descriptions. She thinks of her dead husband as a living presence: "Mike's been gone these five years," she says: "Mike ain't done nothing new, has he?" Out of loss and personal weakness grow her disease, which Marlowe recognizes in his first simile: ". . . the voice dragged itself out of her throat like a sick man getting out of bed." The account of her life that follows is the first in a detective novel to show the consequences of the heroic drinking the genre so often celebrated (*FML*, 20–21).

The cameo most closely related to traditional American folk humor is that of the black clerk who runs the Hotel Sans Souci. When Chandler dropped the casual cynicism that led him to use "nigger," "smoke" and "Harlem sunsets," he could depict blacks with linguistic fidelity. For the clerk, language is a defensive screen against white people: "Brother, I forgit," he says. "Trouble, brother, is something we is fresh out of." He has a repertoire of street-corner and church-house sayings that satisfy the demands of conversation without tipping his hand: "May the Lord receive his soul, brother." "Daid, brother, gathered to the Lawd. Nineteen hundred and thirty-four, maybe thirty-five. I ain't precise on that." "The pursuit of knowledge, brother, is the askin' of many questions" (*FML*, 17–19).

The clerk is, in fact, a kind of sphinx, a sleeping oracle to the white detective: all-seeing and seemingly oblivious, he gives answers only when the detective approaches him correctly. He unmasks falsehood easily, as when Marlowe implies he is from the Hotel Protective Department: " 'A nice name, brother. Clean and cheerful. You're looking right well today. . . . But you ain't no H.P.D. man. Ain't seen one in years.' He unfolded his hands and pointed languidly at the sign. 'I acquired that second-hand, brother, just for the effect.' " As Marlowe leaves, the clerk "folded his hands on the desk exactly where they had been when I came in. His eyes drooped slowly and he appeared to fall asleep. The incident for him was over." He is an emblem of the inscrutability of black society to the white detective (*FML*, 17–19).

Finally there is the Hollywood Indian, Second Planting, who seems today an outlandish creation. But when Chandler arrived in Los Angeles in 1912, it was common to see impoverished Indians drifting from outlying shantytowns into Los Angeles, seeking day-labor in the motion picture industry. Chandler lavishes some of his most concentrated metaphors on Second Planting, at least in part because of the Indian's role in American myth:

His hat was at least two sizes too small and had been perspired in freely by somebody it fitted better than it fitted him. He wore it about where a house wears a wind vane. His collar had the snug fit of a horse-collar and was of about the same shade of dirty brown. A tie dangled outside his buttoned jacket, a black tie which had been tied with a pair of pliers in a knot the size of a pea. Around his bare and magnificent throat, above the dirty collar, he wore a wide piece of black ribbon, like an old woman trying to freshen up her neck.

He had a big flat face and a highbridged fleshy nose that looked as hard as the prow of a cruiser. He had lidless eyes, drooping jowls, the shoulders of a blacksmith and the short and apparent awkward legs of a chimpanzee. I found out later that they were only short.

If he had been cleaned up a little and dressed in a white nightgown, he would have looked like a very wicked Roman senator. (*FML*, 118)

Farewell, Women

Chandler dealt more generously with his female characters in *Farewell* than he had in *The Big Sleep*. There is something to like in both Velma and Anne. Chandler established both as redheads, a type of the genre, then introduced a subtle generic distinction: Velma dyes her hair blonde, becoming another "type," while Anne, knowing the cliché, describes her hair as "auburn."

Anne Riordan, the police chief's daughter who helps Marlowe break the case, is from the mold of Dashiell Hammett's Effie Perrine. She turns up clues, she's a nice girl, and she's available if Marlowe wants her. She is comfortable, as the description of her house makes clear: "It would be a nice room to wear slippers in." Marlowe says sarcastically that "a fellow could settle down here. Move right in. Everything set for him" (*FML*, 160, 157).

But unlike Effie, Anne is aggressive: she orders Marlowe to spend the night, tells him she has a "beautiful figure," and demands to be kissed. It isn't that Marlowe isn't interested. "She came back with the glass and her fingers cold from holding the cold glass touched mine and I held them for a moment and then let them go slowly as you let go of a dream when you wake up with the sun in your face and have been in an enchanted valley." This is clearly "the romantic dream on which love feeds" (*FML*, 158).

But the genre is not about love, said Chandler. As in the case of Mona Mars, coldness signals the ideal, unattainable woman, the girl with the cornflower blue eyes. Marlowe is a knight, a detective. He has a code: to protect innocence. As he tells Lieutenant Randall, "She's a nice girl. Not my type." When Anne tells him point-blank that she has never made love, he shuts his mouth with his hand in order not to trample her naiveté (*FML*, 166).

The responsibility for not harming the innocent or succumbing to the temptation of romance hangs heavily on Marlowe. When Anne asks him to stay the night, Marlowe must become angry; he returns to his quarters with a sense of relief: "I unlocked the door of my apartment and went in and sniffed the smell of it, just standing there, against the door for a little while before I put the light on. A homely smell, a smell of dust and tobacco smoke, the smell of a world where men live, and keep on living" (*FML*, 161).

Marlowe's type, in the sense that she promises some self-knowledge he lacks, is Mrs. Grayle (grail). "I like smooth shiny girls, hardboiled and loaded with sin," he notes. Velma stands first in that file: "Whatever you needed, wherever you happened to be—she had it." She is "a blonde to make a bishop kick a hole in a stained glass window," a combination of the Carmen and Vivian archetypes that Chandler used in *The Big Sleep*. Like Vivian she is classy and clever, like Carmen she is a blonde killer (*FML*, 166, 78).

But Marlowe is wary of Helen Grayle from the beginning. Her eyes are his book: as they harden, soften, or close they provide his clues. In her kiss—"her tongue was a darting snake between her teeth"—he recognizes her biblical ancestor Eve. When he reveals her as Marriott's murderer, Marlowe notes, "Suddenly, without any real change in her, she ceased to be beautiful. She looked merely like a woman who would have been dangerous a hundred years ago, and twenty years ago daring, but who today was just Grade B Hollywood." Her eyes, as

she leaves after killing Malloy, are "a dead grey, like half-frozen
water." This is an important updating of the succubus, for Chandler
here presents evil in terms of Hollywood banality (*FML*, 113, 238,
240).

Yet she is no simple stereotype. Velma is given the characteristics
of Vivian in *The Big Sleep* and engages in pointed repartee with Marlowe, indicating that Chandler respected her. She resembles Mona
Mars in many respects; she has, as Chandler's allusion to Shakespeare
points out, "certain dregs of conscience, but still wanted the money."
She is also the "Lovely" of the title. The novel's final sentence—"You
could see a long way, but not as far as Velma had gone"—indicates
that her life serves as a parable, perhaps of the consequences of social
mobility in America, perhaps of the wages of love.

Metaphor in *Farewell, My Lovely*

With *Farewell, My Lovely* it becomes apparent that a cosmopolitan,
eclectic mind moves Marlowe. Marlowe cannot be an actual detective,
for he lacks verisimilitude; he is rather the vehicle of a superior intelligence, whose breadth of interests and experiences provides his metaphoric palette.

When a reader begins a Marlowe story, he agrees to participate in
a hyperbolic adventure, rather than a mimetic experience. The difference between the reader's experience and Marlowe's world is plastic
and can be stretched in interesting ways. For two decades it had been
stretched in terms of exotic locales, women, crimes, villains, heroes,
and solutions; but Chandler was the first to stretch the genre's language. He showed that hyperbole, overstatement, irony, simile, metaphor, sarcasm, and cliché could be exotic. In allowing the narrator
to stretch the detective novel stylistically, the reader consents to participate in an ironic appreciation of the genre. He is allowed to be
in the action, and above it, on a pseudo-authorial level. This was a
revolutionary step in technique.

The current understanding of metaphor, unlike I. A. Richards's
model of tenor and vehicle, views it as consisting of a focus—the unknown term—and a frame, which is the remainder of the sentence.
Linguist Max Black has shown that the focus is invested with the
"system of associated commonplaces" of the frame. The commonplaces about any subject are known, Black writes, by experts as well
as laymen, for everyone knows "what the man on the street thinks

about the matter." When we say "man is a wolf," we do not mean that he is like the animal; rather we wish to invoke a system of commonplaces that we share about the frame of "wolf." Yet at other times, he notes, the frame can consist of "deviant implications established ad hoc by the writer."[14]

This approach to metaphor is especially useful in dealing with a genre dependent on the election or defeat of popular attitudes for its principal power. And it permits the unpacking of metaphors by attention to the commonplaces they invoke. For example, Marlowe notices, one day, "spring rustling in the air, like a paper bag blowing along a concrete sidewalk." (*FML*, 84). The focus of this simile is spring, with which we are already familiar. The frame is a paper bag blowing down a sidewalk, the sound and friction of one man-made item against another. The system of commonplaces associated with this frame invests spring with a new, deviant meaning. The commonplaces are: that windblown trash occurs in big cities, that paper bags blow along the sidewalk after escaping garbage cans, that there is grit in the air, dirt in the eyes, and disheveled clothes. As readers, we supply the commonplaces that evaluate to "unpleasant," and spring acquires the unexpected value of "urban blight." Unpacking the metaphor further reveals that the focus itself is actually a worn personification: spring "rustles," like a leaf or a woman's petticoats. What the romantic imagination had conceived to "rustle," Chandler ironically reevaluates as blowing trash.

One of the most famous metaphors in the novel is widely misunderstood because the frame is Los Angeles's history. Marlowe tells Lindsay Marriott, "This car sticks out like spats at an Iowa picnic." The car has already been described as "a huge black battleship of a car with chromium trimmings, a coyote tail tied to the Winged Victory on the radiator cap and engraved initials where the emblem should be. The car had a right-hand drive and looked as if it had cost more than the house." The hood ornament identifies the car as a Rolls-Royce. Since the focus is again already known, attention turns to the frame, which is commonly supposed to be a picnic of farmers in rural Iowa (*FML*, 50, 39–40).

However, in the thirties in Los Angeles an "Iowa picnic" meant the annual gathering of the Iowa Society on Iowa Day, 18 January. Held at Bixby Park in Long Beach, these "picnics" attracted as many as 150,000 transplanted Iowans. The Iowans were at once resolutely provincial and politically active; they picnicked by counties, wore buttons with the legend "Hog and Hominy," yet demanded that California politicians court their votes at these gatherings. The Iowans were mostly elderly, like nosy Mrs. Morrison from Mason City, and moved to Los Angeles to retire or because of illness. The only one who might wear spats to an Iowa picnic would be a politician, come to court votes, or an outsider unfamiliar with the Iowans' immediate adoption of California's light clothing.

But the metaphor's frame is even richer and more personal. "Spats" comes from the English "spatterdash," long leggings worn to protect the trouser leg. During their vogue in the 1920s, spats were made of leather and polished to a black gloss. Serving no practical purpose, they typified the dress of dandies, a set vilified by dime detective novels. This subsystem of commonplaces applies equally to Marriott and his car; they stand out in the canyon's brush, a kind of frontier on which he proposes to meet those updated Indians the criminals, just like a dandy but servile politician would at a gathering of old and practically attired voters. Marriott and the politician may have style, but the criminals and the voters call the shots. The metaphor is personal because Chandler, an emigrant, senses the foreignness of both the Rolls-Royce and its American owner to the majority of Los Angelans. He makes a frame that epitomizes the "native" Los Angeles population by its anti-English, anti-dandy attitudes. It also anticipates the denouement because Marriott, a politician of sorts, turns out to be less than persuasive with the crooks.

These examples illustrate an important function of metaphor in Chandler's work. They tend to diminish their subjects rather than increase them in the reader's eyes. In so doing, they imply a power elsewhere that enhances or reduces the status of the subject in question. In a popular genre this power is the central myth, in this case the mythology of knighthood, which draws to itself the power of other things and actors through reductive tropes. For Chandler, metaphor is simply myth writ small. Ironically, by diminishing other things and actors, he reestablishes the myth of knighthood in the post-Einsteinian world.

Critical Reception

His second novel was always Chandler's favorite: "I think *Farewell, My Lovely* is the top," he wrote, "and that I shall never again achieve quite the same combination of ingredients. The bony structure was more solid, the invention less forced and more fluent" (*SL*, 192). The contemporary reviews were good. Will Cuppy wrote in the *New York Herald* that the novel was "the real thing in wickedness and the best hard-boiled mystery in ages." The *New Republic* said "Chandler is a neat craftsman and writes like a breeze."[15]

Most scholars agree that the novel is an extraordinary performance. Philip Durham, the dean of Chandler scholars, called it "the most complex and successfully united work" that Chandler produced, and Stephen Pendo writes that it is "the best of the writer's novels." Mac-Shane thinks it "a much better book than *The Big Sleep*." For Dennis Porter, it has the "characteristic mark of a Chandler novel . . . a quality of extravagance that is present not only in the evocation of decor as here but also in the description of character, in the pungent dialogue, and in the general texture of his prose as well. Such a style applied to characters gives rise to the creation of grotesques often equal in their vividness to those of the great Victorian novelists." Only Peter Wolfe dissents, writing that "the critical reputation of *Farewell* is drastically inflated."[16]

Chapter Six
Whodunits

The High Window

Neither his best nor worst work, *The High Window* and *The Lady in the Lake* are transitional novels. Chandler's earlier powers of comparison are present, and often astonishingly fresh, but frequent authorial intrusions and self-parody indicate his anxiousness to push the genre's limits further, to speak straightforwardly. There are hints of the weightier themes that mark his later work, but he did not provide Marlowe with problems of character to develop them. These novels show instead an increased attention to plot; Chandler had by this point read hundreds of mystery novels, English and American. As several critics have shown, he often came closer to the "whodunit" style of English mystery, especially in these novels, than he cared to admit.

The plot of *The High Window* is an original. It repeats some features of *The Big Sleep*, but integrates them better. Marlowe goes to the mansion of Mrs. Murdock, who hires him to find the Brasher Doubloon. A parody of General Sternwood, she inherited her fortune on the death of Jasper Murdock, who is in turn a parody of Chandler's early nemesis Joseph Dabney (whose newspaper memorials Chandler attributes to Mr. Murdock). Mrs. Murdock thinks her daughter-in-law Linda Conquest stole the doubloon when she ran away. She wants the coin back and an uncontested divorce for her son, Leslie Murdock.

The outsider in the family is blonde Merle Davis, Mrs. Murdock's personal secretary, who is as close to the family as Rusty Regan was to the Sternwoods. She's not only timid but suffers, as Marlowe discovers when he touches her casually, a sexual neurosis: unlike conventional blondes, such as Carmen and Helen Grayle, Merle can't stand men. But she does provide Marlowe with clues: the names of Linda Conquest's friends Lois Magic and Louis Vannier.

Leslie Murdock, like Vivian Regan, comes to Marlowe's office to quiz him. Just as Vivian was in debt to Eddie Mars, Leslie owes

$12,000 to gambler Alex Morny. He suspects Marlowe's mission because he, like Vivian, hides a secret: his father "was a man named Horace Bright who lost his money in the crash and jumped out of his office window." As in *The Big Sleep*, Marlowe has to untangle the circumstances of a death that has already occurred.[1]

Marlowe learns that gambler Morny has married Lois Magic and bought an estate beyond Bel Air. He goes there and questions the chauffeur, the first of many "little people" he befriends. Louis Vannier comes from the backyard and takes Marlowe to see Lois, but she reveals nothing. Marlowe next confronts George Anson Phillips, who has been tailing him. A detective in a jam, Phillips gives Marlowe the key to his apartment. "Just like that," wonders Marlowe, "I could have the key. . . . We were in the same racket." Phillips will serve as Marlowe's analogue, as Regan did in *The Big Sleep* (*HW*, 44).

Downtown, Marlowe visits Elisha Morningstar, a numismatist who called Mrs. Murdock about the doubloon. He says he can produce it for $1,000; but he will be murdered by younger and tougher conmen, just as Geiger was in *The Big Sleep*. As Marlowe leaves, he overhears Morningstar calling Anson, but when Marlowe arrives at Anson's rooms he is dead. Marlowe dupes the building manager into helping him search the rooms: as they go up, a drunken resident tries to pull a gun on the manager, finds the weapon used to kill Anson instead, and is framed for the murder.

Lieutenant Jesse Breeze, who resembles Lieutenant Randall in *Farewell, My Lovely*, and his assistant Lieutenant Spangler, are assigned the case. When Breeze interrogates Marlowe, the latter ironically offers Randall as his character reference. Back at his office, Marlowe receives a small box with the apparent doubloon in it. He calls Mrs. Murdock, telling her of Morningstar's offer and Phillips's death. She says the coin has been returned; Marlowe, baffled, leaves his doubloon at a pawnshop. Then he goes to the Belfont Bldg., a replica of the Santa Monica office in *The Big Sleep*, and finds Morningstar dead.

Breeze and Spangler interrupt Marlowe's chess game at home to grill him a second time. Drinks lessen the tension, but Marlowe delivers a moralistic lecture, tells a specious story about the "Cassidy" shooting, and concludes with a pitch for following the dictates of conscience. Unimpressed, the police give him until noon the next day to reveal all he knows. After they leave, Marlowe gets a call asking him to meet Alex Morny at the Idle Valley Club, which is a replica of Eddie Mars's Cypress Club in *The Big Sleep*.

Marlowe and Morny trade information, but the real payoff is an interview with long-sought Linda Conquest, who sings at the club. She reveals a hatred for Mrs. Murdock that is based on her mistreatment of Merle, for whom Linda has a sisterly concern similar to that of Vivian for Carmen Regan. She adds that when Vannier goes to the Murdocks he always asks for Merle.

The next morning Marlowe tells Mrs. Murdock that he has until noon to solve the case. She calls in Leslie to deliver a rehearsed speech explaining how he stole and returned the coin. Marlowe doesn't believe it, but when he reports to the police two hours late, they surprise him by announcing that the drunk confessed to Phillips's murder. It turns out that a local mafioso who is hiding a fugitive in the building will pay his legal fees if he confesses, and the police like the tidy story.

A call from the manager of his building takes Marlowe to his apartment, where a hysterical Merle Davis says she has killed Vannier. Marlowe calls a doctor to tranquilize and stay with her until he can drive her to her parents in Wichita, Kansas. Over at Vannier's house Marlowe finds the blackmailer shot in the head. By chance he discovers a picture with a negative and two prints behind it of a man leaning out of a high window. The photos show Mrs. Murdock pushing her first husband out a window; on the back Vannier has recorded $11,100 in blackmail money he received. Marlowe hides when Alex Morny and Lois Magic arrive. Each of them suspects the other of a murder that neither committed. Morny declares he is turning Lois in even though he loves her, a scene that echoes the climax of *The Maltese Falcon* and is a bit of parody on Chandler's part.

At his apartment Marlowe finds Merle recovering. He reclaims the doubloon from the pawnshop and confronts Mrs. Murdock. Marlowe tells her a bowdlerized version of the events of 26 April 1933: Merle was the secretary of Horace Bright, who made a pass at her. Given the chance and a bit of insanity, she pushed him out the window. Mrs. Murdock helped Merle avoid charges, and the coroner helped Mrs. Murdock get insurance money by ignoring suspicions of suicide. She confirms this, adding that Merle "blamed herself" and took the blackmail money to Vannier as a form of "penance." Then Marlowe reveals Vannier's death, calling it a suicide. He does not pin her husband's death to Mrs. Murdock; he just asks her to have Merle's suitcase packed.

The truth emerges when Marlowe confronts Leslie, who confesses to stealing the coin in order to copy it with Vannier and an accomplice. Phillips was a dummy they needed to sell the coin to Morningstar, who called Mrs. Murdock to check its authenticity. Phillips got nervous and sent Marlowe the doubloon. Desperate to return it, Leslie contacted Vannier, who gave him a counterfeit. Then Vannier killed Phillips and Morningstar when neither of them could produce the original. Leslie killed Vannier when he tried to increase his hold over the Murdocks by telling the truth: that his mother pushed his father out the window. But Vannier's death was an accident, says Leslie. Not to worry, says Marlowe: nobody's prints are on the gun.

Before they drive to Kansas, Marlowe shows Merle the photo and tells her she did not kill Horace Bright, that Mrs. Murdock used her. After a week of moral refurbishment in the heartland, Merle is rolling piecrusts and kissing Marlowe. "I had a funny feeling as I saw [the] house disappear, as though I had written a poem and it was very good and I had lost it and would never remember it again," notes Marlowe, echoing his "enchanted valley" feeling for Anne Riordan (*HW*, 202).

American Character and Wealth

Although published before *The Lady in The Lake*, *The High Window* is best understood thematically as following it, for its themes are already those of *The Little Sister* and *The Long Goodbye*. Foremost among them is the effect of wealth on the native American character. Chandler had portrayed the wealthy as sick (Carmen, General Sternwood, Mr. Grayle) or unscrupulous (Vivian Sternwood, Helen Grayle) in his two previous novels.

The analysis deepens in *The High Window*. Chandler replaced Rusty Regan, who revealed a potential fate of the detective, with a family servant, Merle Davis, who in name, position, and origin serves as the Young Woman from the Provinces come to seek her fortune in Los Angeles. Chandler cast her as an emigrant from the Midwest because, like Linda Conquest (who is from Sioux Falls, S.D.) the majority of Los Angelans came from there.

Chandler locates the Murdocks in a Pasadena mansion because in the 1930s that community represented wealth as no other did. Unlike General Sternwood, whose values Marlowe respected, there is nothing to admire in port-swilling, tight-fisted, domineering Mrs. Murdock.

General Sternwood and Mr. Grayle created their wealth; Mrs. Murdock killed for hers, just like the criminal who hounds her. Yet the naive Merle, who has been made to shoulder Mrs. Murdock's sin, admires her and secretly loves her son Leslie. Merle is a *captive*, whose dilemma echoes those found in colonial captivity narratives; her Indians are the rich. Eventually she comes to admire them, losing her native cultural sensibility, for which she is smitten, as if by a puritan God, with a species of infertility. Marlowe's mission is to restore the captive maiden to health and civilization.[2]

This theme is buttressed by the death of detective George Anson Phillips. Phillips is a bumbler, a n'er-do-well, in short, a bad "woodsman." He is too innocent, too trusting to survive among the criminals and the rich. Thus Marlowe's wonder: "I could have the key to his apartment and go in and make myself at home. I could wear his slippers and drink his liquor and lift up his carpet and count the thousand dollar bills under it." As the reference implies, Phillips does not understand what men will do for money. He dies at the hands of Vannier, but his death is a consequence of the greed that drives all the rich (*HW*, 44).

Marlowe's discourse on the "Cassidy case," while lamentable artistically, serves to emphasize this theme. The police cover up the murder/suicide of a rich young man and his secretary at the behest of his multimillionaire father. "What the hell difference did it make who shot who?" asks Lieutenant Breeze. "Did you ever stop to think that Cassidy's secretary might have had a mother or a sister or a sweetheart—or all three?" asks Marlowe. "That they had their pride and their faith and their love for a kid who was made out to be a drunken paranoiac because his boss's father had a hundred million dollars?" (*HW*, 92). The captive is an important moral exemplar for his peers back home; the quality of his resistance makes the strength of their values and their God manifest. But wealth suborns even the truth of the captive's deeds, says Chandler, and causes those who remained in the provinces to lose faith.

This innocence stands out by contrast with the novel's varied images of worthlessness, nullity, and void. The most common trope is "nothing." Marlowe sizes up conversation: "There was nothing in that for me." The Belfont Building is "eight stories of nothing in particular." People sit "blankeyed," their faces "empty." Lieutenant Breeze stares "thoughtfully at nothing." The telephone gives "a droning on the wire and beyond that nothing." Marlowe feels "empty," the "dead air doesn't move." Eddie Prue has "a grey face full of nothing." Marlowe closes a door carefully "for no reason at all." This nullity in part reflects Chandler's weariness of the demands of metaphor-making, but it is also an attempt to create a backdrop of nonentity, against which innocence is the only unimpeachable human quality. Like the house of Merle's parents that Marlowe sees in his rearview mirror, innocence is disappearing, corrupted by its attraction to "Idle Valley." Chandler, an old romantic poet, underscores the value of innocence by his comparison of it to a wonderful, lost poem in the last lines of the novel's penultimate chapter.

Changing Characterization

It is not often noticed that the characters of *The High Window* are among Chandler's most realistic. In contrast to the grotesques of *Farewell, My Lovely,* these characters have complex motivations and realistic appearances. Policemen Spangler and Breeze, unlike Nulty and Randall, are real people, not exaggerations. Spangler "wasn't smiling and he wasn't tough, just a big solid man working at his job." Lieutenant Breeze has a cigar-lighting ritual, like Sam Spade's cigarette-rolling routine in *The Maltese Falcon*, that makes Marlowe cautious: "Every motion had been exactly as it had been . . . and exactly as it always would be whenever he lit a cigar. He was that kind of man, and that made him dangerous. Not as dangerous as a brilliant man, but much more dangerous than a quick excitable one like Spangler." Chandler lavishes one of his finest extended similes on Breeze when Marlowe gives him a drink: "he picked the glass up and tasted it and sighed again and shook his head sideways with a half-smile; the way a man does when you give him a drink and he needs it very badly and it is just right and the first swallow is like a peek into a cleaner, sunnier, brighter world" (*HW*, 86, 89, 88).

Chandler's villainess, Mrs. Murdock, has been criticized as unconvincing. Perhaps she is not truly evil, but her blend of pettiness and greed, alcoholism and egotism, becomes despicably familiar. The reader is never quite sure of Marlowe's opinion of her: is she merely difficult, like General Sternwood, or truly malignant? Despite his speech on the value of truth to the police, Marlowe does not insist on her guilt. Instead, she seems strong enough to force him to trade his silence for Merle. When Marlowe last sees her, she is cheating at solitaire again. She remains free at the end because Marlowe can not bring her to justice without destroying what is left of Merle's innocence (*HW*, 181).

Leslie Murdock and Linda Conquest convincingly combine hard-boiled exteriors with sentimental interiors. Leslie is weak, dependent on his mother, and should be eminently hateable for his cruelty to Merle. Yet he isn't: he loves Linda even though she has left him, and for Chandler love always redeems. Appearing late in the novel, Linda seems like the latest in a chorus line of "smooth, shiny girls." But her insightful analysis of Mrs. Murdock and concern for Merle vindicate her.

The least convincing characters are the criminals. Alex Morny is nowhere near as formidable as Eddie Mars or Laird Brunette. Louis Vannier, with his "olive skin, brilliant black eyes" and sideburns is a stereotypical Latin hoodlum. The Italian Mafia, which made its appearance in Los Angeles in the 1930s, is represented in romanticized fashion by Pietro Palermo, of whose taste in dress and interior decor Marlowe approves. But Palermo is just local color: Italians had no roles in Chandler's conception of the American myth, which was a melodrama of native innocence despoiled by native greed.

Shop-Soiled Galahad

In *Farewell, My Lovely* Marlowe was supremely aware of his own hypocrisy, of the paradoxes life presented. In *The High Window* he faces similar situations, but he feels neither remorse nor astonishment. Chandler had tired of holding reality and idealism in the strict tension that good parody demands, with the result that Marlowe's conscience appears to have dulled, his senses to have atrophied.

When he finds Phillips's body, Marlowe chastises himself for looking twice: "Nothing in that, Marlowe, nothing at all." Several times he looks in the mirror and is surprised by the foreignness of his own face, and his tolerance of evil seems greater. That he works on behalf of Mrs. Murdock never bothers Marlowe. He lets Leslie go free. "You mean you're going to let me get away with it?" Leslie asks. "There's no question of morality involved," answers Marlowe. "I'm not a cop nor a common informer nor an officer of the court. You say it was an accident. Okay, it was an accident. I wasn't a witness" (*HW*, 56, 195).

These changes in Marlowe's code are partially masked by his ritual insistence on observing its formal aspects. As always, he is absolutely scrupulous about money. When Mrs. Murdock asks about his "expenses," Marlowe says, "You'll get it all down in black and white. You'll have a chance to object, if you don't like it." His respect for monetary honesty extends to paying Morningstar the five dollars he demands for his information and giving the manager of the Florence Apartments a dime for a beer. As always, Marlowe makes every effort to preserve his client's anonymity, asking only that she tell him the truth. Nor has he shed his suspicion of the police, telling them small lies, such as "I had to go to the dentist," when he is not refusing their requests outright (*HW*, 7, 135).

Marlowe's rescue of Merle Davis, however, emphasizes the detective code more than all the dialogue. Hammett set up a similar situation in *The Dain Curse*: a cult was holding Gabrielle Dain captive and so debilitated her that she couldn't have sex with men. Hammett's detective not only rescued her but restored her sexually, which is exactly what Marlowe does. This is a new paradigm for Chandler, whose knight in previous novels considered robust female sexuality a sure sign of promiscuity. Chandler's solution, like Hammett's, was to put Marlowe's chastity impossibly far above temptation; he moves into a hotel while Merle recuperates in his apartment.

Such sudden embraces of the pure code of knighthood, followed by lapses that excuse Leslie and Mrs. Murdock, create a sense of slackness in the novel. Idealism cannot be tempered by pragmatism or moral ennui and remain idealism unless it is subsequently drop-forged on the anvil of parody. The only reconciling metaphor that Chandler offers is Dr. Carl Moss's sobriquet: "Phil Marlowe . . . the shop-soiled Galahad" (*HW*, 161).

Proletarian Strains

Tough-guy fiction, as Jacques Barzun has commented, "shows the Marxist colouring of its birth years."[3] American fiction in the 1930s was influenced by the Depression, the Russian revolution, and the artistic program of social realism. Writers such as Upton Sinclair united with ideologues like Mike Gold to propose a fiction of the worker, his condition, and problems. Although completely uninterested in this program, Chandler recognized the value of increased sympathy for "the little guy" to a writer working in a popular genre.

Thus Marlowe makes an ally of Alex Morny's chauffeur. He befriends and compliments the elevator operator of the Belfont Bldg. far beyond the requirements of plot. He sends money to "a pathetic old rooster" named Peabody in Sausalito who does handwriting analysis. But Marlowe will have nothing to do with Socialist politics or even unions. When the elevator operator says he works twelve hours a day, Marlowe says "Don't let the union hear you." An odd encounter occurs when a guard stops Marlowe at the entrance to Idle Valley. "And they call this a democracy," hisses Marlowe. "Maybe you got company," replies the man; "I knew a fellow belonged to the John Reed Club. Over in Boyle Heights, it was." Elsewhere in Chandler's work Boyle Heights is synonymous with petty crime. Marlowe and the guard agree that while social revolutions "get in the hands of the wrong people," these people can't be much worse than the rich. Chandler apparently intended to tap the American suspicion of programmatic solutions, which he judged to be deeper than current economic dissatisfactions. All ideologies, including socialism, he implies, are simply sham; nothing could protect workers from the vicissitudes of the Depression (*HW*, 81, 102).

A related motif that Chandler employed over a dozen times in *The High Window* is the statue of the black coachman by the front door of the Murdock mansion. "He looked a little sad, as if he had been waiting there a long time and was getting discouraged." The statue suggests that Marlowe is the "nigger" of the Murdocks; after his interview with Mrs. Murdock he "went over and patted the little Negro on the head again. 'Brother, . . . you and me both.' " Morny's chauffeur, who looks "like an overgrown jockey," repeats the motif, and Morny's Club features an actual Negro in white linen, gold epaulettes, and cap, as well as a customer who curses the bartender as if he were a slave. Marlowe's "That's white of you" to the police indicates that they are all "slaves" in this commonplace. Chandler belabors this motif a dozen times before he realizes "the joke seemed to have worn thin" (*HW*, 2, 103, 178).

Tough Talk

The structure and meaning of repartee are laid bare in *The High Window* to an unusual degree, perhaps because of Chandler's sluggish stylistic performance. His "tough talk" draws on the commonplaces of gangster movies, well-known actors, and other detective novels. Its cardinal values are speed and originality, a notion of virility (discussed by Marlowe and Merle), and smoothness in form and tone. Repartee runs two courses: it can escalate until it results in violence, or both parties can recognize it as a creative game, in which case they try to sustain the contest. In "cracking wise" the meaning of *cracking* is "sudden, unexpected, breaking"; thus "Cap" Shaw, his first editor, gave Chandler's wisecracking style the high accolade of "brittle."

Tough guys never say what they mean in tough talk because tough talk is aggressive metaphor. Ordinarily, as linguist Ted Cohen has shown, the author of a metaphor issues an invitation that his auditor expends mental energy to accept. If successful, they communicate intimately because the metaphor assumes shared commonplaces "inaccessible to all but those who share information about one another's knowledge, beliefs, intentions and attitudes." Keith Newlin notes that Marlowe often uses wisecracks to rob people of their defenses. As Cohen explains, "Sometimes one draws near another in order to deal a penetrating thrust. When the device is a hostile metaphor or a cruel joke requiring much background and effort to understand, it is all the more painful because the victim has been made a complicitor in his own demise."[4]

So Marlowe's repartee is cryptic, forcing his auditor to puzzle out its meaning. This gives him a tactical advantage: the tough guy without verbal resources stands verbally flat-footed, trying to comprehend, and soon withdraws or threatens violence, in which case he automatically loses the contest. The worthy opponent engages in repartee, the delivery of verbal and mental pain. Marlowe keeps the repartee escalating because as Chandler's proxy he can be bested only when the writer permits. Chandler permits only for verisimilitude (and counseled the writers of the Marlowe radio series to do likewise) or to develop other admirable characters (Anne Riordan), but he never allowed the detective to show himself verbally inferior to evil.

All types of trope are permitted in tough talk: metaphor and simile are merely in highest relief. Hyperbole and irony are common, and understatement (even litotes) appears, as well as metonymy and synecdoche. They show that the detective brings unusual resources to the situation. In the case of Marlowe, the resources are not only as great as the interests of Raymond Chandler, ranging from the laws of physics to the plays of Shakespeare, but they illustrate a unified worldview.

Tough talk can furthermore be graded by the system of associated commonplaces to which it refers. The lowest form of tough talk is that copied from the movies. As Marlowe notes of Morny, "Every motion, every gesture, right out of the catalogue." Better opponents, like Linda Conquest, incorporate irony and hyperbole into their repartee. The most challenging are also quick to reply and clever (*HW*, 109).

Since he talks tough, the detective seems to be like the crooks; but he uses tough talk against them for idealistic ends. Language is a kind of Trojan horse, a tool, and the repeated demonstration by Marlowe of its limits is a critique on behalf of idealism. The world presented in tough talk is a competitive, workaday world ruled by proof, profit, physics, and wealth. But the tropes the detective uses in tough talk to best his opponents point to a hidden "world elsewhere," which is more civilized and ample than the one in which they live. As Newlin notes, the wisecracks tend increasingly toward self-parody in *The High Window*, and Marlowe even begins to apologize for them, pointing to a realm of values off the page. This stylistic evocation of idealism is one of Chandler's major triumphs, an aspect of the genre in which he surpassed Hammett.

"No Action, No Likable Characters, No Nothing."

Chandler was the harshest critic of *The High Window*. When he sent it to Knopf, he wrote: "I'm afraid the book is not going to be any good to you. No action, no likable characters, no nothing. The detective does nothing." After its publication he wrote a friend that "*The High Window* was not the striking and original job of work that could be promoted into anything of consequence. Some people liked it better than my other efforts, some people liked it much less. But nobody went into any screaming fits either way." He was particularly depressed that readers took his portrait of the pawnshop owner as anti-Semitic. By the late 1940s and early 1950s he was referring to it as "my worst" and writing "that book is usually considered my weakest effort" (SL, 20, 22, 317). But as Peter Wolfe notes, "Just as he had overrated *Farewell, My Lovely*, so did he underrate *High Window*. A look at the later novel's plot discloses developments presaging artistic growth rather than decline."[5]

The novel "wobbles between burlesque and an expression of anger against ruthless behavior," writes Frank MacShane. "The seriousness of Chandler's theme shows how ambitious he was for the detective novel. It may also explain why he thought he had to exaggerate the jokes and the characters in order to make the book palatable. *The*

High Window has thematic unity and a pace that suggests fresh work. But it is also odd, a curious mixture of elements that seem somewhat uncomfortable together." Jerry Speir scores the weak connection between the stories of the coin's theft and Merle's rescue. "Simple greed," he says of the first plot, "is just not as engrossing as the subtler shades of trust, mistrust, love, power, and mental derangement that Chandler handled so skillfully in the first two novels. While the plot does explore such motivations to a degree, its power is diminished by the secondary status given to the more intriguing relationship between Mrs. Murdock and Miss Davis. Moreover, Chandler's efforts to link these plots are unconvincing."[6]

Stephen Pendo stands alone in praising the novel as "one of the author's structurally superior efforts," although Peter Wolfe is partially in agreement, writing that Marlowe "plays a more active role than he did in *Farewell*, and he displays much more initiative." But he, like MacShane, feels the book is divided in tone and plot, and ends by calling it a "thin, parabolic novel" and "an artistic failure."[7]

The Lady in the Lake

The Lady in the Lake is a much better novel than a log of its composition would indicate. Chandler began it in March 1939; it took him a month to write fifteen pages. He stopped, wrote other stories, fiddled with titles, started *Farewell, My Lovely*, rewrote sections, reverted to the original, and threw out 55,000 words. Four years after he began, in 1943, he finally finished the story. His biographer attributes the book's faults to this "extraordinarily long period of gestation." Based on "Bay City Blues" (1937) and "The Lady in the Lake" (1939), the book resembles Chandler's first two novels in its cannibalization of earlier material, but its structure is by far the best integrated of the three.

The plot of *The Lady in the Lake*, though split between the Bay City and Little Fawn Lake settings, is linked by a carefully worked out motif of mistaken identities. It begins when Derace Kingsley, a cosmetics company executive, hires Marlowe to find his missing wife, Crystal, who has telegraphed from El Paso that she is marrying boyfriend Chris Lavery.

Kingsley acts tough in public, but privately he and Marlowe establish a male camaraderie, which is the dominant tone of the novel. He gives Marlowe a note to Bill Chess, the caretaker of the cabin where

Crystal was last seen, and warns that she is a kleptomaniac: in his business he can't have scandal. His secretary Adrienne Fromsett, an update of Anne Riordan, provides Lavery's address. But Lavery says he's not marrying Crystal, hasn't seen her, and didn't go to El Paso.

As he leaves, Marlowe notices the house of Dr. Albert Almore, one of Chandler's dope-dealing doctors. He sits and watches Almore watch him until Lieutenant Degarmo arrives. Degarmo acts tough, but he and Marlowe also fall into camaraderie. Marlowe phones Kingsley, who says Almore was his wife's doctor and that Mrs. Almore committed suicide.

At Little Fawn Lake, Marlowe meets manic-depressive Bill Chess, who has a lame leg, a wandering eye, and a problem with alcohol. After Marlowe gets him drunk, Chess tells how his wife Muriel caught him in Crystal Kingsley's bed. Then, he says, both blondes—"same size and weight, same type"—disappeared. After checking Kingsley's cabin, they discover Muriel's body submerged in the lake, a "mistaken identity" that drives the rest of the plot. Marlowe fetches Deputy Sheriff Jim Patton, who takes Chess in.

After dinner Marlowe learns that an L.A. cop recently showed around a photo of "Mildred Haviland" that resembled Muriel Chess. Marlowe goes back to search Chess's cabin, but Patton is inside and demands an explanation. They exchange ideas, and Patton shows an anklet he found. Marlowe pretends to leave, then searches the cabin as he intended: he finds a locket inscribed "Al to Mildred." He gives this to Patton and drives to the San Bernardino hotel where Crystal left her car. Mistaking her photo, employees confirm that Crystal confronted Chris Lavery in the lobby.

On the second day Marlowe returns to Lavery's house. He finds the landlady, Mrs. Fallbrook, wandering about, gun in hand. She fools Marlowe by giving him her gun. By the time he finds Lavery dead in the shower, she's gone. Marlowe meets Kingsley and shows him the gun; he says it looks like Crystal's. Miss Fromsett tells Marlowe that Almore's wife, sensitive about his reputation, gambled at Lou Condy's casino and died of a drug overdose. Marlowe returns to Lavery's house and calls the Bay City police, one of whom reveals that they covered up the Almore "suicide." When Marlowe asks Captain Webber and Degarmo about this, Degarmo hits him.

Next Marlowe visits Florence Almore's parents, who hired a detective named Talley to investigate their daughter's "suicide." Talley was framed for drunk driving and sent to prison, they say; Mildred

Haviland was Almore's nurse. Talley's wife won't talk to Marlowe; when he leaves, the Bay City police are waiting to frame him just as they did Talley. They work Marlowe over and take him to the new Bay City jail. Then Degarmo takes him to see Captain Webber, who explains that Talley stole evidence in the Almore case: a green velvet dancing shoe.

After he's released, Marlowe calls Kingsley, who has heard from Crystal. Marlowe, wearing Kingsley's scarf, is to give her $500. At the drop-off, Marlowe won't give "Crystal" the money until she answers questions. They go to her apartment. When Marlowe identifies her as Mildred Haviland/Muriel Chess/Mrs. Fallbrook, she pulls a gun on him, and he is sapped by a man behind a curtain.

Marlowe wakes up on a gin-soaked bed beside Muriel, who is the victim of a sex crime. As police knock at the door, he climbs out a bathroom window into the next apartment. Dressed in the clothes of the absent owner, Marlowe saunters out and runs into Degarmo, who smuggles him past the other police, ostensibly to solve the crime and claim credit for himself. When Degarmo heads for the country rather than headquarters, Marlowe produces Kingsley's scarf, implying it will frame Kingsley for "Crystal's" murder. They decide to confront him; Marlowe thinks he may be at Little Fawn Lake and calls Patton, who confirms the guess.

As Degarmo and Marlowe drive through the night and early morning of the novel's third day, they share the camaraderie of travel and exchange details on the Almore cover-up. Muriel killed Mrs. Almore with Dr. Almore's aid. When she needed money to escape life with Bill Chess, she decided to bribe Almore, but he sent Degarmo, her ex-husband, still in love with her, to dissuade her. Stringing Degarmo along, Marlowe asks him not to hang murders on Kingsley that he doesn't deserve.

Patton is waiting for them, but when they enter the cabin, Kingsley is obviously innocent and reveals that he gave Marlowe the scarf. In the denouement Marlowe explains that Muriel killed Crystal and towed the corpse underwater. She knew Chess would be blamed for her death, but that Crystal would be missed, so she planned a false trail, but accidentally met Lavery, who knew her. She took him with her to El Paso, then killed him when he posed a threat. She had returned to "edit" the job when Marlowe met her as Mrs. Fallbrook. Degarmo, who loved and hated her, killed Muriel and set up Marlowe for the sex crime.

Patton won't let Degarmo leave and shoots the gun out of his hand, but Degarmo barges out anyway. Patton phones to set up roadblocks; soon he receives word that Degarmo refused to stop for sentries at the dam. The last guard shot at his car, which sailed off a cliff.

Mellowing Marlowe

The mistaken-identity motif and background of a society preoccupied by World War II divert attention from the mellowing of Marlowe's character. He may resemble the Marlowe of old, but he engages in less repartee, has one fight, and never pulls his gun. He is sapped once and roughed up by the cops once. Chandler's opinion that only international unity against the Axis powers could save civilization led him to paint a more cooperative world. Figures of authority—the police, the client, politicians—whom he previously characterized as hostile to Marlowe, now share information with him or at worst are merely gruff. There are no professional criminals, only Chris Lavery, a blackmailer willing to talk to Marlowe (unlike Vannier), and Mildred Haviland, a neurotic who appears only once.

The law is represented by Sheriff Jim Patton ("I liked everything about him"), the human embodiment of the natural virtue of Puma Lake, and by the Bay City police, who have improved since *Farewell, My Lovely*; Marlowe's arrest by Cooney and Dobbs is gentle compared to that by Blane and Galbraith. The tone of camaraderie even permits Marlowe to get along with Degarmo, one of the villains.

Unlike previous incarnations, the mellow Marlowe states his business and names his client when pressed; in return others share information with him. In fact, Marlowe is given most of his leads, rather than developing them. This mellowing also shows in his actions. He demands a $100 retainer in his interview with Kingsley, then retracts the demand: "That's just something I said when you were tramping on me." Pumping Bill Chess for information, he notes, "I like to drink, but not when people are using me for a diary." When Chess says "The hell with you," Marlowe says, "All right, the hell with me." When Patton says that Marlowe must do a lot of divorce work, he lets it go.[8]

Marlowe is aging and losing his hostility. "I brushed my hair and looked at the gray in it. There was getting to be plenty of gray in it. The face under the hair had a sick look. I didn't like the face at all."

To Degarmo he says, "I'm all done with hating you . . . It's all washed out of me. I hate people hard, but I don't hate them very long." He thinks of himself as "a nice enough fellow, in an ingenuous sort of way." This Marlowe is two-thirds of the way to the portrayal in *The Long Goodbye* that renewed the genre (*LL*, 125, 197, 94).

Wicked Women

The camaraderie of this novel is shared by members of a Round Table of Beleaguered Knights, who are beset by unfaithful blondes. Kingsley is worried sick about Crystal, even though he wants a divorce; he drinks himself unconscious when he learns of her death. Bill Chess is simple, but not schizophrenic. He believes he's betrayed Muriel: "I was too much of a skunk to play ball with her." He knows he has violated the code of knighthood, as he confesses: "I'm getting away with something. Us boys can be so wrong about those little things, can't we? I'm not getting away with anything at all." But it turns out that Chess is naive compared to the blonde he believes he has betrayed. Even Degarmo is no mere tough: Muriel made life "a small private hell for him." In turn he "loved her and hated her, . . . too much of a cop to let her get away with any more murders, and not enough of a cop to pull her in." The only male not welcome at the Round Table is Lavery, a gigolo, with whom Marlowe trades his toughest repartee (*LL*, 31, 33, 212).

Tempting the Knights is a Chapel Perilous full of "neat little blondes," all promiscuous as cats. This danger is established at the outset by Marlowe's leering at the "neat little blonde" PBX operator and Kingsley's brotherly confession of his wife's loose morals. It is developed further by Chess's account of his sex life at Little Fawn Lake and the descriptions by bellhops at the San Bernardino hotel: "these small blondes are so much of a pattern that a change of clothes or light or makeup makes them all alike or all different." The archetypal blonde that Marlowe seeks dresses in black and white, a reminder that fidelity is an issue of right or wrong. "Too much loving, too much drinking, too much proximity," says Marlowe, "ending in a savage hatred and a murderous impulse and death" (*LL*, 77, 125).

Perhaps recognizing his own habit of pairing central female characters (Carmen/Vivian, Velma/Anne, Linda/Merle), Chandler made Crystal Kingsley and Mildred Haviland twins not only in appearance, but in morality: both bed Lavery and Chess. Mildred betrays Lavery,

Chess, and the two Als: Degarmo, Almore. Crystal betrays Kingsley and Chess.

Foiling the blondes is Adrienne Fromsett, who dresses in a "steel grey business suit . . . and a man's tie." She has dark hair and "rather severe eyebrows and large dark eyes." The descriptions suggest she is one of the guys, like Anne Riordan. She dislikes perfume, and when Kingsley makes her a gift of Gillerlain Regal, she protests that she cannot afford it: this distrust of sham and her economic parsimony signal the reader that she, like Marlowe, has a code. Equally indicative is her condemnation of Florence Almore as "one of these slinky glittering females who laugh too much and sprawl all over their chairs, showing a great deal of leg. A very light blonde with a high color" (*LL*, 2, 105–6).

If sexual promiscuity has a heavy price, which Crystal's death illustrates, so does unreciprocated love, as Degarmo's death shows. The description of Crystal's bloated body rising, disfigured, from the depths of Little Fawn Lake, is a masterpiece of moral imagery. Ornamented in green jade, the color and gem that symbolized Carmen Sternwood's nymphomania, Crystal is the Arthurian "lady of the lake," who gives the knight a glimpse of his fate should he follow the course of promiscuity: this vision is his most valuable weapon. "She's not nice to look at," Marlowe tells Patton, echoing a line from Hammett's "The Scorched Face." In both stories sexual promiscuity leads to the death of women. When Marlowe meets Muriel disguised as Mrs. Fallbrook, he describes her as "like the erring wife in East Lynne," a reference to Mrs. Henry Wood's 1861 melodrama, in which unfaithful Isabelle Vane disguises herself. Muriel's death provides a second graphic warning against promiscuity: "Her mouth was open and a swollen tongue filled it to overflowing. Her eyes bulged and the whites of them were not white. Across her naked belly four angry scratches leered crimson red against the whiteness of flesh. Deep angry scratches, gouged out by four bitter fingernails" (*LL*, 90, 173). On the other hand, Degarmo is allowed to commit suicide because his motive is essentially one of frustrated chivalry. This is an example of what R. W. Lid has termed "Chandler's failure to sustain a morally dispassionate view of his characters."[9]

Another inconsistency is Chandler's treatment of the gigolo Lavery, who beds Mildred, Crystal, and Adrienne Fromsett, and dies for his promiscuity. Chandler attempts to elicit sympathy for him when Marlowe discovers his body; he uses Marlowe's point of view to put

the reader in Lavery's shoes: "Nice efficient work. You have just
finished shaving and stripped for the shower and you are leaning in
against the shower curtain and adjusting the temperature of the
water. The door opens behind you and somebody comes in. The
somebody appears to have been a woman. She has a gun. You look at
the gun and she shoots it" (*LL*, 93). If the lesson is not clear: Marlowe's alter ego Talley, having discovered the truth, falls for Muriel
and plans blackmail with her, only to find himself framed by Degarmo and sent to jail. It is this perilous pattern that Marlowe is following when he is arrested and framed.

When the reader meets Muriel, the Loathly Lady, she only mum-
bles about her life being a "hopeless tangle." There is no measure of
her attractive power. She kills many people, in coldly premeditated
ways, and is killed by the first man she wronged, Degarmo, in a
feigned sex crime. Present crimes, for Chandler, are always rooted in
the past: Marlowe enters the case to uncover original sin. In this case,
the original sin was leaving Degarmo, who loved her; the primal
murder was killing Florence, to marry Dr. Almore.

Metaphor in *The Lady in the Lake*

The Lady in the Lake recovers some of the metaphoric brilliance of
the earlier novels, especially in applying motifs to characters consis-
tently. Bill Chess, for example, is carrying a "double-bitted axe"
when Marlowe meets him, and he laughs "like a tractor backfiring."
Then he shuts his mouth "as tight as a trap", and Marlowe says
"You're slipping your clutch." Describing his adultery with Crystal,
Chess says he felt "as smooth as a new piston head." The reader un-
derstands that Chess is a machine, with two faces or gears, and is thus
not too surprised that he "hit himself in the face with all his
strength." He simply has a gear missing, as his bad leg shows. One
of Chandler's most outrageous puns is Chess's explanation of his lust:
"After a while a guy like me, a common no good guy like me, he
wants to feel a leg. Some other leg" (*LL*, 28–29, 30, 33, 50, 31).

The metaphors describing Sheriff Patton establish him as a figure
in harmony with nature: he looks "as dangerous as a squirrel and
much less nervous," holding his "head sideways, like a watchful
bird." Then the frames become historical: he wears "a leather jerkin
which must have been new once, say about the time of Grover Cleveland's first term." Finally he is associated with the American frontier;

Marlowe leaves him "moving his mind around with the ponderous energy of a homesteader digging up a stump." He has the native ingenuity, in other words, to solve problems with the bare minimum. Patton thus inherits the frontiersman's mantle (*LL*, 42, 62, 60, 73).

Animalization, as a mode of metaphor, is not new in Chandler, but it is one of the dominant frames in this novel. As always, he favors cats over dogs: "She looked playful and eager, but not quite sure of herself, like a new kitten in a house where they don't care much about kittens." Marlowe and Chess are "as friendly as puppies." Refrigerators "growl," speedboats make a "barking roar." Mr. and Mrs. Grayson "pointed like bird dogs" twice; the canary in their lobby lives in "a cage as big as a dog-house." After being sapped, Marlowe decides to stay "on all fours a while, sniffing like a dog who can't finish his dinner but hates to leave it." Later he shakes "Degarmo's hard paw." Handshakes are always detailed—"as rough as a rasp," "like an iceman's tongs," "as stiff as an eggshell" "like a towel rack"—because of Chandler's sensitive hands (*LL*, 37, 85, 51, 127, 126, 173, 200).

Echoes of World War II

In a short story cannibalized for this novel Chandler featured a Japanese spy and a villain who cried "Heil Hitler!" before shooting himself. Though he removed these ridiculous characters, the war remains an important background and contributes to what some have perceived as a "somber" tone. It also vindicates Chandler of the charge, often leveled, that his work was purely escapist, having no relation to the realities of the Depression or World War II.

The Lady in the Lake opens with a reference to rubber sidewalk blocks being taken up in front of the Treloar Building on Olive Street—a donation to the government war effort. Elsewhere Marlowe notes the Bay City police are not saving tire rubber when they speed to Lavery's house. Mrs. Fallbrook tells Marlowe she walks "to save my tires for the government." Such admonitions to conserve were a common face of the war, but there were others: the dimmed lights in Bay City, the laughing soldiers Marlowe sees in the Peacock Bar, and the sentries he passes as he crosses Puma Dam. Al Norgaard (of *Farewell, My Lovely*) is in the military police, says Degarmo, wishing he were too. Another cop in the story is signing up: "I'll be in the army in two weeks," he tells Marlowe, explaining his sarcasm about the

Bay City police. The war also informs Marlowe's discovery of an important clue: "Silk slips were not being left behind that year, not by any woman in her senses" (*LL*, 114, 88, 150, 26, 198, 24, 141, 70).

The war also accounts for the somber color schemes. Long partial to gray, Chandler let it dominate the descriptions. Kingsley wears gray, Miss Fromsett dresses in gray, her apartment is furnished in gray, the Gillerlain offices have "dull silver" walls, and a midwestern family, the Graysons, are the victims of Mildred's first murder. The body Marlowe finds in the lake is "a blotch of gray dough, a nightmare with human hair on it (*LL*, 40).

Sheriff Patton's name, of course, echoes that of General George Patton, a California native. The war also frames some metaphors: Marlowe notes in a junkyard that the "automobiles lay in grotesque designs, like a modern battlefield" (*LL*, 137).

High Praise

It is difficult to dislike *The Lady in the Lake*. Jacques Barzun calls it "Chandler's masterpiece," and other scholars have judged it "his finest" and "most engaging." Ross Macdonald ranked the novel among his favorites and underscored his opinion by reworking the setting and characters in *The Zebra-Striped Hearse*.

Philip Durham, first to notice the counterpoint of rural and urban settings, wrote that "the unsaintly Santa Monica, the town of brutality and evil, was contrasted with the purity of the mountains, where the Sierra Madres cast their spell on the man of action." Expanding on this view, Jerry Speir writes that "evil has escaped the city and reveals itself as a product of individual avarice and passion capable of carrying on quite well outside the modern urban wilderness." It has found its way, he says, "even into society's remotest, most idyllic hideaways." Many have simply enjoyed the descriptions of nature; as Clive James noted, "Chandler's descriptive powers are at their height in *The Lady in the Lake*."[10]

Unlike most readers, who are surprised by the unfolding personalities of Degarmo and Muriel, MacShane sees *The Lady in the Lake* as a dark book "because it concentrates on those who are caught up in the system of Southern California, instead of those who direct it. They are the foot soldiers of society rather than the picturesque eccentrics of *The High Window* to whom the system belongs. . . . What Chandler shows us is a society of men and women trying somehow to keep their lives together, but always under pressure and therefore susceptible to violence."[11]

Wolfe notes that the lyric descriptions of nature and the intricacies of plot, more typical of the English detective novel, serve to advance a distinctly California theme: "the effects of image worship. In our competitive, middle-class society, people must maintain a clean facade, a requirement necessitating cosmetics and, in dire cases, murder. Kingsley, we recall, hired Marlowe to begin with to protect his good name, i.e., his job and reputation. Kingsley also manufactures cosmetics. Besides pandering to vanity, cosmetics are used in impersonations." Besides the villainess, others touched by this motif include Marlowe, arrested when he uses the pomade of H. G. Talbot and sapped after wearing Kingsley's scarf, and Miss Fromsett, whose cologne unfairly implicates her in Lavery's murder. Chandler used this motif to update a long-standing theme also recognized by Wolfe: "Chandler's people, like Scott Fitzgerald's, come to grief because they try to relive the past. Moose Malloy thought he could recover the love he believed he shared with Velma. . . . Degarmo's obsession with Muriel neglects the truth" that she is no longer his wife.[12]

Chapter Seven
Darkening Vision

The Little Sister

In *The Little Sister* Chandler returned to a problem he had touched lightly in *The High Window*: why do emigrants lose their native American virtue in Los Angeles? The earlier book used the captivity motif to assign the blame to the rich. But after three years in Hollywood Chandler blamed the "awful money hunger" of the emigrants themselves and the film industry's encouragement of "acting" on all levels of life. When California broke its "promise of a life of ease," acting made retributive violence easier.

Chandler's emigrants are the Quest family of Manhattan, Kansas. Mousy-looking Orfamay, a medical receptionist back home, hires Marlowe to find her brother Orrin, a priggish photographer who has disappeared into Los Angeles. Both are marked by their frugal mother, whose piety preceded the needs of her dying husband. Both hate their older sister Leila, the black sheep, who escaped this midwestern Gothic. Orfamay says she is using her vacation and savings to find errant Orrin.

She leaves Marlowe a $20 deposit and Orrin's last address. But he has left his shabby room in Bay City, and Marlowe finds George F. Hicks there, donning a toupee and packing up to leave. On the way out Marlowe finds the drunken manager (who tried to phone a Dr. Vincent Lagardie when Marlowe arrived) with an ice pick in his neck. When Marlowe calls Lagardie (an emigrant from Cleveland), he feigns ignorance.

Orfamay coquettishly demands her money back when Marlowe reports no progress. He returns it, kisses her, and gets the money again. A man who needs "something kept in a safe place" calls Marlowe from the Van Nuys Hotel. Suspicious, Marlowe checks with Flack, the house detective, before going up to the room. Inside a blonde woman saps him: when he recovers, he finds Hicks with an ice pick in his neck and a camera shop claim ticket under his toupee.

Marlowe brings Flack up, then Lieutenants Christy French and Fred Beifus arrive. They mention that Sunny Moe Stein's men used ice picks in Brooklyn, but that Stein was murdered by Weepy Moyer. Marlowe catches Flack stealing from the dead man's wallet, but lets him go in return for the license number of the blonde's car. With this number he finds the address of actress Mavis Weld (Leila Quest), whom he calls up. But he reaches her friend, the "Mexican" actress Dolores Gonzales (another Clevelander), who invites him over and tries to seduce him. When Mavis appears, she won't give Marlowe any information, but slaps, kisses, and throws glasses at him. On his way out Marlowe runs into gambler Steelgrave (Weepy Moyer), a third Clevelander.

As he drives back, Marlowe thinks about Los Angeles and its hucksters, then goes to a movie in which Mavis Weld has a role. At his office he finds Joseph P. Toad and his junky nephew, modeled on Gutman and Wilmer in *The Maltese Falcon*. Marlowe turns down their offer of $500 to forget the case. Then he gets three phone calls: Toad says Marlowe should check with Sherry Ballou, Mavis Weld's agent; Dolores Gonzales wants to seduce him; and Orfamay says she's heard from Orrin. When she appears, she's wearing perfume, the first of several cosmetic experiments that show how "acting" supplants native values.

Marlowe turns in his camera shop claim check, receiving a photo of Mavis Weld and Steelgrave at the Dancers Club. A reporter helps him date the photo to the day when Stein was killed and Steelgrave was supposedly in jail. Next he sees agent Sherry Ballou, who has all the habits of Billy Wilder that Chandler despised. He retains Marlowe to investigate the blackmail of Weld. On his way to see Weld at her studio, Marlowe meets movie mogul Jules Oppenheimer, who delights in allowing his dogs to pee wherever they want. "Fifteen hundred theatres is all you need," he says. This is apparently meant to be Louis B. Mayer, whose MGM owned 1,500 theaters and whom Chandler (without knowing him) disliked greatly. In the studio Marlowe waits while Weld and two actors bicker their way through a scene. She refuses to cooperate.

Orfamay again tells Marlowe she has heard from Orrin; he's staying with Dr. Lagardie. Marlowe questions Lagardie, who denies knowing Quest and dopes Marlowe with a drugged cigarette. When he wakes up, Orrin falls dead into his arms, an ice pick in his hand. Next Dolores proposes to Marlowe that they blackmail Mavis together. Marlowe declines, going to see French, Beifus, and Lieutenant Maglashan, who tries to intimidate him.

Dolores says Mavis is in trouble and picks up Marlowe at his office. They drive through Hollywood, Marlowe lecturing on how crime has infected Los Angeles. In Bel Air they meet a citizens' roadblock, but talk their way through it to Steelgrave's hilltop gambling club. Inside, Marlowe finds Mavis with Steelgrave's body. She claims she killed him.

Mavis says that Orrin took the photo and blackmailed her, but that she kept his identity from Steelgrave. She wants to turn herself in, believing that not even Oppenheimer can save her. Marlowe sends her out the back way and arranges a cover-up, refusing to tell Beifus and French anything when they arrive. French lectures him and takes Marlowe downtown, where he's interrogated. The next morning Mavis Weld and her high-priced lawyer are in District Attorney Endicott's office when Marlowe arrives. The lawyer argues that the photo cannot be used as evidence because no witness will link it to Steelgrave's murder. Weld and Marlowe go free.

Orfamay, in dowdy dress, arrives at Marlowe's office to say she's going home, but first she wants to know how Orrin died. Marlowe explains more than she anticipated: Leila was the child of a first marriage, Orfamay and Orrin of a second. The new wife and children were "ashamed" that Leila consorted with gangsters and decided to make her pay. Snatching Orfamay's handbag, Marlowe exposes the $1,000 she collected from Steelgrave and explains how she sold out her brother. He accuses her of shooting Steelgrave. She admits only that she wanted a cut of Orrin's blackmail money.

Marlowe visits Dolores and exposes her as Dr. Lagardie's wife from Cleveland; she admits goading Orfamay into killing Steelgrave, who had jilted her for Mavis. To get revenge she seduced Orrin and got him to kill Stein. With the photo he took, they framed Steelgrave, but when he closed in on them, she killed Orrin. As Marlowe is phoning the police, Lagardie arrives. Still in love with his ex-wife, he kills her and then himself.

Thematic Confusion

The Little Sister is highly regarded by critics who see Chandler as a social critic of Southern California. They cite the lectures against modern civilization that he put in the mouths of his characters and the classic allusions: Orfamay, like Orpheus, makes a descent into hell when she visits Southern California. Her Eurydice is Orrin. There is even a stray allusion to *Antigone*. Unfortunately neither the lectures nor the allusions mesh with the novel's plot, and the complete corruption of the Quest family, which might unite them, is not revealed until late, when its magnitude overwhelms the reader. Orfamay doesn't appear often enough to carry the weight of the theme and is balanced anyway by Leila's admirable qualities. This leaves Dolores Gonzales as the novel's major villainess.

Stripped of its plot, *The Little Sister* blames moral decay in Los Angeles on emigrants from the American heartland. Chandler makes the Quests symbolic in name (Orfamay, Orrin, and Leila are pioneer names, Quest signifies "the American dream") and in geographic origin: they come from Kansas. Demographically, they represent the wave of emigrants from the Midwest and Dust Bowl states who moved to California between 1900 and 1940. The immorality that overtakes them is the product of a fatal mix of flaws: once land-hungry pioneers, disciplined by family and church, they conceive themselves anew in a land without strictures, where exotic, even rapacious, behavior is rewarded. Their flaws stem from pioneer materialism and a failure to understand that human obligations persevere in the urban world, even in the absence of church and family.

This analysis has no relation to historic reality. Emigrants arrived in California with strong, often extended family units. It was the abundance of geographically dispersed single-family housing and the jobs in agricultural piecework, at far-flung manufacturing sites, and in acting (all depending on individuals rather than groups) that caused the breakdown of emigrant families. John Steinbeck's picture of the destruction of the Joad family in *The Grapes of Wrath* is far more accurate than Chandler's account.

On the other hand, Chandler's rendering of the morality at work in Hollywood itself is not only insightful, but based, ironically, on an update of pioneer values. He reserves his best treatment for Leila: unlike her Kansas family, she adapts to the demands of her new environment. She accommodates herself to inferior actresses, working her way up through the ranks. She is brave and perseveres through crises, searching Hicks's room after his murder and sapping Marlowe. She is loyal to envious Dolores and a brother and sister who blackmail her. She is even willing to end her career to protect Orfamay. Like Marlowe, she has standards, is independent, and engages in repartee.

The flaws of Hollywood devolve, therefore, upon another outsider, Dolores Gonzales, whose every thought and utterance illustrate the "acting" motif that colors the movie industry. But her character is so overwrought as to be comic. Hollywood has no real representative in the novel, only cameo appearances by Sherry Ballou and Jules Oppenheimer that show advanced cases of the self-indulgence and the divorce from reality to which "acting" leads. The "Hollywood disease" and its course are detailed in lectures, none more pointed than this:

> Wonderful what Hollywood will do to a nobody. It will make a radiant glamour queen out of a drab little wench who ought to be ironing a truck driver's shirts, a he-man hero with shining eyes and brilliant smile reeking of sexual charm out of some overgrown kid who was meant to go to work with a lunchbox. Out of a Texas carhop with the literacy of a character in a comic strip it will make an international courtesan, married six times to six millionaires and so blase and decadent at the end of it that her idea of a thrill is to seduce a furniture mover in a sweaty undershirt.[1]

The most revealing lecture links Chandler's critique to traditional American values; it is the one that Marlowe gives to Dolores as they drive to Steelgrave's casino:

> "I used to like this town," I said, just to be saying something and not to be thinking too hard. "A long time ago. There were trees along Wilshire Boulevard. Beverly Hills was a country town. Westwood was bare hills and lots offering at eleven hundred dollars and no takers. Hollywood was a bunch of frame houses on the interurban line. Los Angeles was just a big dry sunny place with ugly homes and no style, but goodhearted and peaceful. It had the climate they just yap about now. People used to sleep out on porches. Little groups who thought they were intellectual used to call it the Athens of America. It wasn't that, but it wasn't a neon-lighted slum either."
> ....
> "Now we get characters like this Steelgrave owning restaurants. We get guys like that fat boy that bawled me out back there. We've got the big money, the sharp shooters, the percentage workers, the fast-dollar boys, the hoodlums out of New York and Chicago and Detroit—and Cleveland. We've got the flash restaurants and nightclubs they run, and the hotels and apartment houses they own, and the grifters and con men and female bandits that live in them. The luxury trades, the pansy decorators, the Lesbian dress designers, the riffraff of a big hard-boiled city with no more personality than a paper cup. Out in the fancy suburbs dear old Dad is reading the sports page in front of a picure window, with his shoes off, thinking he is high

class because he has a three-car garage. Mom is in front of her princess
dresser trying to paint the suitcases out from under her eyes. And Junior is
clamped onto the telephone calling up a succession of high school girls that
talk pidgeon English and carry contraceptives in their make-up kit." (*LS*,
202–3)

This passage, often cited to show how Marlowe sours on Los Angeles as he ages, is more important as a manifestation of nostalgia for
the unspoiled frontier, typical of popular fiction after 1910, and the
detective genre's conservative underpinnings. People used to sleep
outside, but now everything is spoiled. Chandler does not admit, as
he did in *The Big Sleep*, that the pioneers who settled Los Angeles also
destroyed it. Instead he blames the decline on "outsiders" from the
big cities of the East. But the Quests, expected to bear the burden of
this theme, are from a small midwestern town.

The integrity of the theme also suffers from Chandler's elitist critique of contemporary culture. He resents the use the average man
has made of material progress. Marlowe complains that the quotidian
citizen sits before his picture window reading the sports page, gloat-
ing over his three-car garage. He hasn't created Athens in America.
Does Marlowe want him to? Aren't Dad's values also Marlowe's? Isn't
Dad Chandler's reader? Deprecating Mom's attempt "to paint the
suitcases out from under her eyes," Chandler attacks the American
woman for responding to the value that society places on youth and
appearance; but readers note that Chandler's work places tremendous
value on feminine youth and appearance. In Marlowe's condemnation
of Junior's licentious girlfriends, however, the conflict surfaces most
clearly, for Marlowe is a devotee of "smooth, shiny girls, hard-boiled
and loaded with sin." Nor does he worry about their grammar when
he calls them on the phone.

"Written in a Bad Mood"

The Little Sister is a critical conundrum. Almost every scholar recognizes its flaws: the Hollywood sketches are extraneous, the metaphors the flattest in any Chandler novel, the plot confused and
interrupted by lectures. Yet like Nathanael West's *The Day of the Lo-
cust* and F. Scott Fitzgerald's *The Last Tycoon*, books Chandler ad-
mired, *The Little Sister* is a "Hollywood novel" and that alone attracts
attention. In spite of the flaws, some have found the pathology of Los

Angeles that Chandler proposes quite convincing. Herbert Ruhm called it "the best novel about Hollywood" ever written. On the other hand, Philip Durham wrote that it was "in no sense a 'Hollywood novel.' "[2]

Chandler was his own severest critic. He was tired of Marlowe: "He's getting self-conscious, trying to live up to his reputation among the quasi-intellectuals." Chandler's years in Hollywood left a bitterness that not even the novel assuaged: "The people and the events in this book are not entirely fictional. Some of the events happened . . . and certain of the characters were suggested by real persons, both living and dead." And he was dispirited by the mechanics as he wrote: "There is nothing in it but style and dialogue and characters. The plot creaks like a broken shutter in an October wind." Later he wrote to a correspondent: "It's the only book of mine I have actively disliked. It was written in a bad mood and I think that comes through" (*SL*, 122, 158).[3]

MacShane calls *The Little Sister* "an overripe book." It has the familiar touches, he wrote, "but there is no organic development beyond what he had written before. The little sister, Orfamay Quest, is an extension of Merle Davis . . . but unlike Merle, Orfamay is part of a family that includes a confidence trickster who tries to blackmail his other sister, a rising movie star, who in turn is a friend of a prostitute and a racketeer. These relationships give Chandler an opportunity to write about the interlocking levels of Hollywood society," says MacShane, which he ignores. "Most of the scenes that deal with the movies are just decorative. . . . [They] read as though Chandler were trying to avenge himself for all the irritations he had endured while working in Hollywood."[4]

Those who insist on the novel's seriousness point to the parodies of grail motifs and chivalric romance, to the effects of the Hollywood mentality on individuals, and to Marlowe's bitter insight that he is part of this society. William Ruehlmann calls it "Chandler's strongest—and angriest—book," a reading that Jerry Speir seconds: "Beyond its black foreboding, *The Little Sister* is also a considerably better work of fiction than is generally credited. In its complications of family, organized crime, and Hollywood, it achieves a panorama of the modern condition which is new for Chandler. And in its discovery of ways to demonstrate Marlowe's connection with the human weaknesses on which the story turns, it provides new insight into his central character."[5]

The Long Goodbye

The Long Goodbye is Chandler's most ambitious and highly acclaimed novel. Like *The Little Sister*, it is an attempt to use the detective novel as a vehicle for social comment. This had been done before—Dashiell Hammett's *Red Harvest* and *The Glass Key* are examples—but not as well as Chandler did it. Written while Cissy was dying, *The Long Goodbye* reaches a level of emotional intensity never seen before in the genre. It features a wholly original plot and a cast of credible characters, all of whose actions contribute to the central theme—the alienation of modern man—while preserving the traditional functions of the genre and role of the detective as a knight.

Longer and slower paced than his previous work, the novel opens with an explanation of how Marlowe meets and befriends Terry Lennox. Initially Marlowe takes him home and sobers him up after he passes out and his disgusted ex-wife Sylvia abandons him at The Dancers Club. Marlowe is intrigued by Lennox's politeness and English accent, his affability and pride. Months later he spots Lennox again, drunk on a Hollywood sidewalk, and runs him home for another meal, then provides traveling money to Las Vegas. Lennox sends repayment and remarries Sylvia, after which Marlowe shares an occasional drink with him (gimlets are his favorite). One day Lennox accuses Sylvia of infidelity. "You talk too damn much, and it's too damn much about you," says Marlowe, walking out.

Lennox then appears at Marlowe's house at 5 A.M. demanding to be driven to the Tijuana airport. It appears that he has killed Sylvia, but Marlowe drives him to Tijuana and declines to call the police. "I know you didn't kill her," he says. "You're wrong about that," replies Lennox. When Marlowe gets home, Sergeant Green and Detective Dayton are waiting: Sylvia Lennox is dead, her face beaten in with a statuette. Marlowe won't answer questions, so they take him in. He marks time in the felony cellblock rather than cooperate with Sewell Endicott, a lawyer sent by millionaire Harlan Potter, Sylvia's father.

The D. A. claims that Lennox went to Otatoclan, Mexico, wrote a full confession, then shot himself. Marlowe still won't talk, so they release him. He gets a ride home from a reporter who suggests that a cover-up is going on. The impression grows when Endicott calls and tells him to be quiet, a warning repeated by Mendy Menendez, an old friend of Lennox. He explains that Lennox was in the English army and captured by the Nazis during World War II. Then Marlowe gets a letter from Lennox, mailed in mysterious circumstances, waffling on his role in the murder. It contains a $5,000 bill.

A second plot line begins when Howard Spencer, a publisher's representative, calls up. He wants Marlowe to babysit hack novelist Roger Wade (Chandler's self-portrait). The alcoholic writer, prone to violence, can't finish his novel and is currently missing. His stunning blonde wife Eileen provides Marlowe with a note about "Dr. V" and information on Wade's stays on drunk farms. Marlowe first turns down, then accepts the job.

From an old friend in The Carne Organization, a big detective agency, Marlowe gets the file on doctors who treat drunks. He finds three suspects. One, Dr. Verringer, is about to sell his "artist's colony" so that he can support a manic-depressive named Earl. The others don't pan out. Marlowe eats dinner, then returns to Verringer's. Spying in a window, he spots Wade and saves him from crazy Earl. At Wade's house he collects a kiss from Eileen and learns that she knew Sylvia Lennox, which links the plots.

During the lull that follows, Marlowe has a gimlet in Terry Lennox's memory and meets Linda Loring, Sylvia's sister. They argue about her father, Harlan Potter, who wants the case closed, and about who killed Terry. But a respectful friendship develops. When Wade has a cocktail party, Linda and the insufferable Dr. Loring are among the unhappy couples present; he causes a scene when he accuses Wade of sleeping with his wife.

Wade takes Marlowe aside and offers him $1,000 a month to be his nanny, but Marlowe, although he admires Wade's aplomb in handling Loring, doesn't like the writer's ego. Nor is he impressed, later on, by Eileen Wade's romantic story of the true love she lost when she was young.

A week later Wade calls Marlowe for help. Marlowe finds him collapsed on his lawn, Eileen smoking a cigarette in the doorway. Marlowe and Candy, the butler, put Wade to bed. When Eileen goes to bed, Candy suggests that Marlowe follow. Instead he collects Wade's drunken notes, attempting to gain insight into his problems. A shot rings out, and Marlowe finds Roger and Eileen struggling over a gun. Wade says he tried to commit suicide: Marlowe says he lacks the courage and doses him with Demerol. Then Eileen invites Marlowe into her bed, and he almost follows, but Candy peeks in the door.

When Linda Loring and Marlowe next discuss the case, she asks him to meet her father. Harlan Potter wants the case closed, but Marlowe politely refuses. Later Wade calls, apologizes for his drunk, and invites Marlowe to lunch. The friend at Carne calls to report that Lennox used to call himself Paul Marston.

Wade looks healthy and his wife is out, so Marlowe mentions Wade's affair with Sylvia Lennox. Upset, Wade begins to drink heavily, while Marlowe sits on the patio, not wanting to abet his alcoholism. The doorbell rings; Eileen has forgotten her keys. They have tea and look in on the sleeping Wade—who is dead. Marlowe's friend Lieutenant Ohls, who handles the case, reads it as a suicide, but Eileen accuses Marlowe. At the inquest, he has to cross-examine Candy, who says Marlowe slept with Eileen, to prove his innocence. Next Marlowe learns about Paul Marston's time in the English Army. The friend at Carne helps with research in England. Then Marlowe and Spencer visit Eileen: Marlowe reveals that she was married to Lennox when she married Wade. She claims that he was lost in the war, but admits to recognizing him in Idle Valley. She spied on Wade and Sylvia, but insists that Wade killed Sylvia. When Marlowe catches her in lies, she runs to her room. He tells Spencer that she killed both Sylvia and Wade; he wants to call the police, but Marlowe stops him.

During the night Eileen overdoses on Demerol, leaving a complete confession. The authorities decide to give it to the D.A., knowing he will smother an inquest on orders from Harlan Potter. But they leak a copy to Marlowe, who gives it to a reporter and clears Lennox's name. Then Linda Loring calls, announcing her divorce and asking Marlowe to go to Paris. He begs off and goes home, where Menendez is waiting to beat him up. But it is Menendez who gets beat up: his hired thugs turn out to be disguised policemen sent by Lieutenant Ohls.

Marlowe and Linda Loring spend the night drinking champagne and making love. Marlowe refuses to marry her and become a kept man. The next day he checks a detail in Lennox's letter with Randy Starr, who promises to answer via emissary. The emissary, Senor Maioranos (Mr. Better-years), is Terry Lennox, his face darkened. He and Marlowe talk but the old affection is gone. As Marlowe said of Linda Loring's departure, "to say goodbye is to die a little."

Technique and Style in *The Long Goodbye*

For many readers *The Long Goodbye* seems a retreat from the cornucopia of tropes characteristic of Chandler's earlier work, and as such a disappointment. These devices are still evident, though not in the earlier quantities. But in other respects *The Long Goodbye* is technically superior to his preceding work.

The greatest change in *The Long Goodbye* is in plot and pace. Most of Chandler's novels were patched together from short stories, with the seams showing variously. *The Long Goodbye* is whole cloth, progressing at a leisurely pace to an unexpected but appropriate conclusion. There are no loose ends, and the mystery—despite Chandler's remark that he didn't care if it was fairly obvious—is adequately preserved. The theme develops over the entire novel but is given its complete meaning only in the last pages. The motif of the robber baron and his two licentious daughters is one Chandler used in *The Big Sleep*, but by placing it deeper in the background he made foreground incidents dominate the reader's attention. In the didactic asides, less obtrusive because of the leisurely pace, he called attention to the powers behind Los Angeles society, of which the paradigm is Harlan Potter.

Chandler's metaphors fall into the same categories that he used earlier: relations of space and weight, death and disease, household objects, cats and dogs. Individual metaphors are as striking as ever: Sylvia Lennox is so cold that "a slice of spumoni wouldn't have melted on her," Terry Lennox has eyes "like holes poked in a snowbank," and Captain Gregorius has a "stare that would have frozen a fresh-baked potato." As Peter Wolfe notes, Chandler expanded his range with synecdoche (" 'Well, that's one way of doing it,' I told the white coat"), litotes ("Ellen Wade materialized beside me in a pale blue something which did her no harm"), and even zeugma ("the light went off, and so did I").[6]

There are still metaphors in series, a trademark of Chandler's early style, but they serve to establish the novel's dominant tone and theme: "The house was leaking guests out into the evening air now. Voices were fading, cars were starting, goodbyes were bouncing around like rubber balls. I went to the french windows and out onto a flagged terrace. The ground sloped towards the lake which was as motionless as a sleeping cat" (*LG*, 147).

But for a Chandler novel, metaphor is noticeably absent, producing a sense of flatness. The diminution was deliberate, for Chandler had grown disgusted with his tropes: "Goddamn silly simile. Writers. Everything has to be like something else. My head is as fluffy as whipped cream but not as sweet. More similes. I could vomit just thinking about the lousy racket." In the same note Wade reprimands himself: "Three adjectives, you lousy writer. Can't you even stream-of-consciousness you louse without getting it in three adjectives for Chrissake?" Roger Wade, the historical romance writer, is an alter ego of Chandler's who must be put to death; the traits of his writing are suppressed as much as possible (*LG*, 165, 167).

In place of the old style Chandler offers one that is slower, less hyperbolic, sometimes objective, and sometimes unabashedly sentimental. Marlowe's description of the felony cells shows what Chandler sought in the objective mode:

> Cell No. 3 in the felony tank has two bunks, Pullman style, but the tank was not very full and I had the cell to myself. In the felony tank they treat you pretty well. You get two blankets, neither dirty nor clean, and a lumpy mattress two inches thick which goes over crisscrossed metal slats. There is a flush toilet, a washbasin, paper towels and gritty gray soap. The cell block is clean and doesn't smell of disinfectant. The trusties do the work. The supply of trusties is always ample. (*LG*, 40)

The long digressions and moralistic lectures may be seen as a weakness, but as MacShane notes, that is a matter of personal preference. Some of them, such as the following one on blondes, contain the novel's sharpest observations:

> There are blondes and blondes and it is almost a joke word nowadays. All blondes have their points, except perhaps the metallic ones who are as blond as a Zulu under the bleach and as to disposition as soft as a sidewalk. There is the small cute blonde who cheeps and twitters, and the big statuesque blonde who straight-arms you with an ice-blue glare. There is the blonde who gives you the up-from-under look and smells lovely and shimmers and hangs on your arm and is always very very tired when you take her home. She makes that helpless gesture and has that goddamned headache and you would like to slug her except that you are glad you found out about the headache before you invested too much time and money and hope in her. Because the headache will always be there, a weapon that never wears out and is as deadly as the bravo's rapier or Lucrezia's poison vial. (*LG*, 72)

These lectures are distributed among the characters, to avoid the appearance that Marlowe has become an ideologue or cynic. So Bernie Ohls expostulates on the evils of crime and reporter Lonnie Morgan on the evils of newspaper power: Chandler tried to make the theme rise from a range of characters.

There are passages that show Chandler in top form, such as the parallelism used to describe Marlowe's reaction to Detective Dayton: "Maybe I was tired and irritable. Maybe I felt a little guilty. I could learn to hate this guy without even knowing him. I could just look at him across the width of a cafeteria and want to kick his teeth in." In the following transitional passage, one month passes in nineteen words:

[Sewell Endicott] was frowning as I opened the door, but I thought it was an honest frown of puzzlement. Or maybe he was trying to remember how it looked outside the hotel and whether there was a mailbox there.

It was another wheel to start turning—no more. It turned for a solid month before anything came up.

Then on a certain Friday morning I found a stranger waiting for me in my office. (*LG*, 30, 304)

Three Portraits of Chandler

Natasha Spender, an insightful friend of Chandler's during his final years, wrote that there were three distinct self-portraits in the novel. "He wrote *The Long Goodbye* as Cissy lay dying. . . . It may well reflect the interior dialogues between facets of his own personality as he looked back upon their long life together, which he was soon to lose. Afterwards his London conversations strikingly resembled the dialogue of all three characters in turn."

Like Terry Lennox, Raymond was a young ex-soldier in the early twenties, battle-scarred and scared, whose pride was that "of a man who has nothing else."
. . . .
Like that of Roger Wade, the successful, middle-aged, alcoholic and egocentric writer, Raymond's drunken stream of consciousness could also at bad moments be full of self-hatred, writer's angst and sarcastic hostility. . . . Wade's wife echoes Cissy in saying, "He was a good actor—most writers are." Like Raymond himself, Wade is childless and says, "If I had a ten-year-old kid, which God forbid, the brat would be asking me, 'What are you running away from when you drink, Daddy?' "
. . . .
Marlowe, of course, represents Chandler's ideal self, the conscience which punished the Roger Wade within him though not without commendation for achievement (for Wade in the book is "a bit of a bastard and maybe a

bit of a genius too"), and befriended the Terry Lennox within, not without censure.

....

All three characters were drinkers, like Raymond himself, two of them disintegrating and despairing, for only the ideal-self Marlowe shows a disposition towards integrity. As aspects of Raymond's own character their dominance veered with his mood, Roger Wade his bad self, Philip Marlowe his "good self" and Terry Lennox his anxious one.[7]

This analysis is buttressed by other details in the text. When Lennox returns, he calls himself Senor Maioranos, a rendering in Spanish of *mayor años* (better years). Lennox represents Chandler's youth, the years before World War I when he embraced the romantic dream of "cornflower blue eyes." Marlowe's last words to him are "So long, Senor Maioranos. Nice to have known you—however briefly." Lennox is also linked to Marlowe when Eileen Wade, noting that Marlowe's initials are those of Paul Marston, throws herself in his arms and says "All these years I have kept myself for you."

Marlowe is linked to Wade when the writer notes that "A good man died for me once," which refers not only to Wade's assumption that he killed Sylvia and Lennox took the blame, but also to the young romantic who died in the process of becoming a pulp novelist. Later on Wade, "fighting for control" of his face, denies knowing anyone named Paul Marston. That Wade and Lennox never appear together is not an accident of plot, but a psychological impossibility. Both are "missing" when Spencer tries to hire Marlowe, both blaming themselves for a death neither caused: that a woman is the murderess and author of their self-doubt is, of course, a theme dating to Chandler's earliest work (*LG*, 311, 173, 168, 206).

Roger Wade is the object of Marlowe's scorn and occasional admiration. Wade invokes Lennox when he tries to hire Marlowe: "I'm asking you as a friend. You did more than that for Lennox." Later he taunts Marlowe on the same basis, "Yeah, call the police . . . like you did on Terry Lennox." Marlowe invests as much of himself in Wade as he does in Lennox. He may detest the corruption of Idle Valley and the "sea of self-pity" in which Wade lives, but after the incident with Dr. Loring he notes: "Wade seemed to have enough control to handle himself if he really wanted to. He had done all right with Loring." "I guess maybe I feel a little responsibility for him by now," Marlowe admits to Eileen. "Your husband is a guy who can take a long hard look at himself and see what is there. It's not a very common gift. Most people go through life using up half their energy trying to protect a dignity they never had" (*LG*, 143, 171, 147, 153).

Marlowe knows the faults of both Lennox and Wade: like both, he is a womanizer and a heavy drinker. His sentimentality at times borders on the self-pity of Roger Wade; his sense of honor and willingness to make sacrifices for others recall Lennox's quiet dignity and wartime heroism. "Part of me wanted to get out and stay out" of Wade's life, he says, "but this was the part I never listened to." What differentiates Marlowe and serves as the crucible of the theme is his code, which is severely tested. As he says, "There is no trap so deadly as the trap you set for yourself" (*LG*, 204, 69).

Marlowe's Code in *The Long Goodbye*

Despite his sentimentality, Marlowe is still faithful to a code. He displays absolute honesty in matters of money. He refuses to spend Terry Lennox's $5,000 bill when he doesn't feel he has earned it; nor does he charge Roger Wade for his services. On the other hand, he pays a high price for the services he must get from The Carne Organization. The idea of money as a medium of honor extends to human relations, for Marlowe remarks, "You bought a lot of me, Terry" and "I owned a piece of him. I had invested time and money in him." The cynical connotation is entirely consonant with the worldview the novel expresses. If "money value" is the ubiquitous measure, then absolute honesty in exchange is the only remaining virtue.

A second tenet of Marlowe's code is absolute independence. Marlowe is the original small businessman. He could be making more money, like George Peters, working for Carne: "He had offered me a job once, but I never got desperate enough to take it" (*LG*, 91). Carne's gray offices remind Marlowe of a cellblock. He takes pride in his ability to survive in a rough-and-tumble marketplace. Rather than take money from people who can solve their own problems, Marlowe suggests that they do for themselves. He turns down Linda Loring's offer of marriage and millions. He turns down Harlan Potter's offer of business, and refuses to be intimidated by anyone. Marlowe needs his hunger and his isolation to stay independent of the large organizations that increasingly dominate his world.

Marlowe also honors the bond of friendship. He goes to jail or suffers the cops instead of betraying friends. He acts on unspoken commitments to Lennox and Wade, to Eileen and Linda. This is the point tested by the novel's action, and Marlowe finally decides that the code as a whole is more important than this one point. He suspends his involvement with friends who are dishonest, threaten his independence, or deny the truth.

Finally, Marlowe is always in search of the truth, whatever appearances suggest; thus his low tolerance for self-aggrandizement, self-pity, and other forms of egotism that he finds increasingly common: they obscure the truth.

Marlowe often appears lax in his code, allowing the police to spit in his face, sleeping with one married woman and nearly with another. These incidents, rather than spelling hypocrisy, unite him with the world he scrutinizes and make more anguished the conclusion he reaches. His only real lapse is pointed out by Bernie Ohls late in the novel: he permits Eileen to commit suicide, obscuring forever the true details of Sylvia's murder in order to clear Lennox's name.

Theme in *The Long Goodbye*

The world consists of huge enterprises—the press, the law, the courts, the police, the criminals—forming a monolith in which good and evil are indistinguishable. Chandler unites them when he reveals that captain of industry and press baron Harlan Potter owns a vacation home next to that of Nevada gambling chief Chris Mady. The implication is that they consult: Potter can have thugs dispatched to Los Angeles to beat up Marlowe. The corruption reaches from the wealthy and organized crime through the press and lawyers such as Endicott to politicians like Sheriff Petersen and cops like Gregorius. The cells of corruption that Chandler previously located in Bay City and Hollywood have enveloped Los Angeles. All Marlowe can do is refuse to be a part of the disease.

Distributed through the novel are asides in which various characters, including Harlan Potter, expound on the nature of this world. Chandler put one of the most important of these in the mouth of his chief villain:

We live in what is called a democracy, rule by the majority of the people. A fine ideal if it could be made to work. The people elect, but the party machines nominate, and the party machines to be effective must spend a great deal of money. Somebody has to give it to them, and that somebody, whether it be an individual, a financial group, a trade union or what have you, expects some consideration in return. . . .

I regard [newspapers] as a constant menace to whatever privacy we have left. Their constant yelping about a free press means, with a few honorable exceptions, freedom to peddle scandal, crime, sex, sensationalism, hate, innuendo, and the political and financial uses of propaganda. A newspaper is a business out to make money. . . .

In large quantities [money] tends to have a life of its own, even a conscience of its own. The power of money becomes very difficult to control. Man has always been a venal animal. The growth of populations, the huge costs of wars, the incessant pressure of confiscatory taxation—all these things make him more and more venal. The average man is tired and scared, and a tired, scared man can't afford ideals. He has to buy food for his family. . . . You can't expect quality from people whose lives are a subjection to a lack of quality. You can't expect quality with mass production. You don't want it because it lasts too long. So you substitute styling, which is a commercial swindle intended to produce artificial obsolescence. (*LG*, 190–91)

The rest of the book makes clear that this is the dominant worldview. Ohls echoes it near the end. Lonnie Morgan of the *Observer* says that "Newspapers are owned and published by rich men. Rich men all belong to the same club. Sure there's competition—hard tough competition for circulation, for newsbeats, for exclusive stories. Just so long as it doesn't damage the prestige and privilege and position of the owners" (*LG*, 54). Marlowe says that Sheriff Petersen, modeled on perennial Los Angeles police chief James Edgar Davis, "had the impassive poise of a cigar store Indian and about the same kind of brains. But nobody had ever called him a crook. There had been crooks in his department and they had fooled him as well as they had fooled the public, but none of the crookedness rubbed off on Sheriff Petersen. . . . Sheriff Petersen just went right on getting re-elected, a living testimonial to the fact that you can hold an important public office forever in our country with no qualifications for it but a clean nose, a photogenic face, and a close mouth. If on top of that you look good on a horse, you are unbeatable" (*LG*, 219).

The last quarter of the novel is an unrelieved litany on the banality of corruption: Chandler looses his fury at public officials, businessmen, lawyers, the press, advertising, the police, and gambling. Harlan Potter is simply Chandler's stalking horse in articulating a worldview that Marlowe accepts as a given but refuses to join (*LG*, 224, 227, 259, 273, 277, 288–89).

In the world these digressions sketch, men are alienated from their institutions and from each other. *The Long Goodbye* abounds in descriptions of alienation: Terry Lennox is a "lost dog" says Sylvia in the opening scene, and "her voice slid away a lot farther." When Marlowe touches Lennox, "he came awake slowly as if it was a long way from where he was to where I was." His apartment contains no "photograph or a personal article of any kind." In jail, Marlowe notes "a man has no personality. He is a minor disposal problem and a few entries on reports." Marlowe is hardly exempt: "I thought about Terry Lennox in a detached sort of way. He was already receding into the distance." Even Marlowe's old friendship with Bernie Ohls has gone sour. Alienation is not only the general atmosphere, but typifies relations between men and women: Dr. and Linda Loring, Eileen and Roger Wade, Terry and Sylvia Lennox, Edelweiss and his wife, "Kitten" and her husband, are all unhappy. The rich of Idle Valley are most alienated of all. Holding the reins of society's institutions, they feel empty. They have no children. Their distress takes the symbolic form of alcoholism, which permeates the novel (*LG*, 2, 4, 26, 57).

The realm of the theme is therefore that of these questions: What is a man's relation to other men in such a world? How far is he responsible to them? What is his responsibility to himself? What allegiance does he owe institutions, abstract principles, the truth?

It gradually becomes clear that the virus under Chandler's microscope is egotism. Its embodiment is Roger Wade, who leaves these notes when he passes out: "I have such a beautiful love for myself—and the sweet part of it—no rivals" and "I do not care to be in love with myself and there is no longer anyone else for me to be in love with." Egotism is the animating passion of gangster Mendy Menendez, to whom Marlowe says, "You're just sitting there looking at yourself," and of Dr. Loring, who makes scenes at cocktail parties to attract attention. It typifies Harlan Potter, who acts as if he could "make a phone call to God and cancel" civilization, and Sheriff Petersen, who "just sat at his desk looking sternly at the suspect, showing his profile to the camera." Its ultimate expression is the manic-depressive Earl, "an actor without an audience . . . putting on a show all by himself and loving every minute of it." Yet without ego there is no chance for civilization; egotism sustains the concept of a personal honor, as Marlowe is the first to admit. "I'm in here for me," he says in jail (*LG*, 166, 87, 64, 193, 219, 114, 44).

Opposed to ego is the claim of each man on every other man, the duty to family, the bond of friendship, a concern for others. The fabric of obligation originates in Terry Lennox, who in disappearing reveals the destructive power of its various forms. During the war Lennox saved the lives of Mendy Menendez and Roger Starr, neither of whom could pay him back. He was Eileen's lover, but she refused to recognize him when he was disfigured. Marlowe is also caught in Lennox's web: "I had invested time and money in him, and three days in the icehouse, not to mention a slug on the jaw and a punch in the neck that I felt every time I swallowed. Now he was dead and I couldn't even give him back his five hundred bucks" (*LG*, 58).

The middle ground between ego and obligation is pointed out by Marlowe's response when Eileen compliments his fidelity to Lennox: "This keeping faith . . . is something even a fool doesn't do twice." The novel, as Harlan Potter might say, tracks an investment that Marlowe makes which steadily depreciates. It points out the *necessity* of investment, of belief in other human beings, against all odds and against probable defeat. Loyalty is necessary, says Chandler, though not immediately productive. Investing in others is investing in oneself, a chance to extend the domain of a civilization one enjoys.

Lennox pushes Marlowe's policy of investing in his beliefs to the limit. When Marlowe says "I know you didn't kill her" and Lennox responds "I'm sorry . . . But you're wrong about that," the reader feels Marlowe has been deluded. But Marlowe continues to believe in Lennox's innocence. As the denouement shows, Lennox *did not* kill his wife; when he said so to Marlowe, he was speaking metaphorically of his moral obligation to her, his failure as a husband and a human being. He killed her by abandoning her to her own devices. Ironically, while Marlowe is vindicated with regard to the murder, he himself is betrayed by Lennox in the same way.

The novel takes its title from the French bon mot with which Chandler sums up Marlowe's night with Linda Loring: "To say goodbye is to die a little" (*LG*, 300). The long goodbye is the tortuous course of the fading friendship between Marlowe and Lennox, two denizens of the realm of gray morality. It finally dies because, as Marlowe tells Lennox, "You're a moral defeatist."

The *Maioranos* of Marlowe

Although Chandler said after *The Little Sister* that his hero had become "self-conscious," there is every indication that for *The Long*

Goodbye he reconsidered Marlowe's character thoroughly, bringing it up to date. On 19 April 1951 he wrote a correspondent a five-page letter detailing the nuances of Marlowe's taste, character, and living conditions minutely. Among the new details: Marlowe was born in Santa Rosa, attended the University of Oregon, and would best be played by Cary Grant.

In the novel Marlowe still works on the sixth floor of the Cahuenga Building, still smokes a bulldog pipe, still plays chess. But he lives in a spacious house with a breakfast nook on Yucca Avenue in Laurel Canyon, a step up the social ladder. His house is surrounded by tall bushes trimmed by a Japanese gardener. He cooks Canadian bacon and makes French drip coffee in the morning and owns a complete set of the California Penal Code.

Outside the house Marlowe carries a short-barreled .32 and uses flat-point cartridges. He is not as quick to fight as he was in earlier novels, nor does he recover from punishment as fast as he used to. He is more often caught off guard by younger men. So he fights dirty, planting a foot in Mendy Menendez's stomach and a knee in his face. But he still has a "canned paragraph" on his life for the inquiring:

> I'm a licensed private investigator and have been for quite a while. I'm a lone wolf, unmarried, getting middle-aged, and not rich. I've been in jail more than once and I don't do divorce business. I like liquor and women and chess and a few other things. The cops don't like me too well, but I know a couple I get along with. I'm a native son, born in Santa Rosa, both parents dead, no brothers or sisters, and when I get knocked off in a dark alley sometime, if it happens, as it could to anyone in my business, and to plenty of people in any business or no business at all these days, nobody will feel that the bottom has dropped out of his or her life. (*LG*, 74)

Contributing to the updated Marlowe is a background of "departures." The old Marlowe was a master of situations in which "a man with a gun comes in the door." The new Marlowe is a man leaving or watching others leave. Chandler ends an exceptional number of the early and middle chapters with departures from rooms, conversations, or situations. They are the tonic chords in a novel whose later chapters increasingly end in the major of goodbye: "But all a man named Marlowe wanted from it was out. And fast." "He drifted out of the office like something blown by the wind." "Cops never say goodbye.

They're always hoping to see you again in the lineup." "To say good-bye is to die a little." "I never saw any of them again—except the cops. No way has yet been invented to say goodbye to them." (*LG*, 179, 275, 278, 300, 312)

The meaning of these goodbyes is summed up by Marlowe at the end of chapter 38:

> I was as hollow and empty as the spaces between the stars. When I got home I mixed a stiff one and stood by the open window in the living room and sipped it and listened to the groundswell of the traffic on Laurel Canyon Boulevard and looked at the glare of the big angry city hanging over the shoulder of the hills through which the boulevard had been cut. Far off the banshee wail of police or fire sirens rose and fell, never for very long completely silent. Twenty-four hours a day somebody is running, somebody else is trying to catch him. Out there in the night of a thousand crimes people were dying, being maimed, cut by flying glass, crushed against steering wheels or under heavy tires. People were being beaten, robbed, strangled, raped, and murdered. People were hungry, sick; bored, desperate with loneliness or remorse or fear, angry, cruel, feverish, shaken by sobs. A city no worse than others, a city rich and vigorous and full of pride, a city lost and beaten and full of emptiness.
>
> It all depends on where you sit and what your own private score is. I didn't have one. I didn't care. (*LG*, 224)

Critical Reception

Of *The Long Goodbye* Chandler wrote: "I didn't care whether the mystery was fairly obvious, but I cared about the people, about this strange corrupt world we live in, and how any man who tried to be honest looks in the end either sentimental or plain foolish" (*SL*, 315). Almost every critic has recognized the revolution Chandler wrought in the genre.

In MacShane's view *The Long Goodbye* is "the vision of a complete novelist" in the European sense, and put Chandler in the company of writers such as Hemingway, Faulkner, Dreiser, and Steinbeck. Focusing on Chandler's extraordinary new range in the novel, Speir writes that it is "at once his most autobiographical work and his boldest attempt to exceed the confines of the detective mystery. . . . Unlike any of its predecessors, it takes on the whole modern society as its subject." William F. Nolan called it Chandler's "finest, most mature

writing achievement." Jerry Palmer judges it "one of the half-dozen
best thrillers ever written," and Peter Wolfe writes that *"The Long
Goodbye* gave the American murder mystery a resonance it had never
enjoyed before. Taking fictional crime away from the mob and drop-
ping it into the family, the book also anticipated the best work of
Ross Macdonald."[8]

Chapter Eight
The True Romance

Playback

Chandler ended his publishing career on the same romantic note that characterized the poems and essays that he wrote for the *Academy* fifty years earlier in London. *Playback*, his last novel, is upbeat, optimistic, and, if critics are correct, a disheartening performance.

Chandler wrote the story originally in 1947 as a filmscript for Universal, combining the plot lines of the short stories "I'll be Waiting" and "Guns at Cyrano's." Financial reverses prevented Universal from filming the project, and Chandler picked it up again in the early fifties. Halfway through he stopped to write *The Long Goodbye*. When he finished *Playback* in 1958 it did not resemble the filmscript. Improbable and cornball, *Playback* is notable chiefly as evidence of Chandler's determination to carry on a creative life after Cissy's death.

The slapstick plot begins when lawyer Clyde Umney hires Marlowe to tail Eleanor King. Marlowe overtakes her in the coffee shop of Union Station, where arch-cad Larry Mitchell intimidates her with a news clipping: "He was California from the tips of his port wine loafers to the buttoned and tieless brown and yellow checked shirt." King reboards the train, with Marlowe following, and travels to San Diego. Marlowe tails her cab to the Rancho Descansado in the resort of Esmeralda, modeled on La Jolla.[1]

By pretending to be her ex-husband, Marlowe gets a room next to his subject, who registers as Betty Mayfield. "I'll always be waiting," he says mournfully to the clerk, an allusion to the short story. Listening through the common wall, he overhears Mitchell try to blackmail Mayfield, then leave. Marlowe rings her doorbell. After he's inside, Betty pulls a gun. He calms her, but Mitchell returns and in the scuffle Mayfield hits Marlowe with a bottle. He wakes up under an ice pack in his own room; outside is a Kansas City detective named Goble, who is looking for Mitchell.

Betty flees but with the aid of a helpful cabbie, Marlowe finds her dining at The Glass Room. Outside he notices Clark Brandon's big car. Inside he finds Mayfield and the sottish Mitchell, who slaps Betty and creates a scene until Brandon forces him to leave. Marlowe tails Mayfield and Brandon to the latter's room at the Casa del Poniente.

In the middle of the night, Mayfield appears at Marlowe's door, saying she has killed Mitchell. When they return to her room, Betty falls asleep and Marlowe can't find any body. He drives to Los Angeles to talk to Umney, then has a date with the blonde secretary, Miss Vermilyea, that ranks as one of the most ridiculous love scenes ever written.

Back in Esmeralda, Marlowe spirits Mayfield off for a candid talk, but she claims not to know what the fuss is about. Since Mitchell is missing now, Marlowe disbelieves. "All right, I'm a liar, I've always been a liar," she says, echoing Brigid in *The Maltese Falcon*. At this Marlowe "glanced in the rear view mirror" apparently at Dashiell Hammett (*P*, 88).

Marlowe confronts Goble, the rube detective who has been tailing him, then cons the garageman at the hotel, who tells him to drop by his shack for a candid talk. Upstairs Marlowe meets Javonen, the hotel detective, who reveals nothing. Afterwards elderly Henry Clarendon IV (Chandler's self-portrait) explains that Mitchell is a gigolo and blackmailer who lives off rich women at the hotel. Marlowe meets Mayfield in the bar, and she gives him, again, the traveler's checks that have passed back and forth so many times that they become a leitmotif.

At the garageman's shack Marlowe finds the man has hung himself. Marlowe goes to the police. Captain Alessandro is not only honest and polite: he believes Marlowe, doesn't demand to know his client, and reveals that Mitchell's car has been found.

Back in Marlowe's room a thug hired by Brandon has beaten Goble and tied him to the bed. Marlowe enters with a tire iron and breaks the intruder's wrists. After the police formalities, he has a drink with Mayfield, tells her that Mitchell is dead, and asks what is going on. She dissembles, then cries "Take me. I'm yours—all of me is yours."

In the morning Captain Alessandro summons Marlowe: Henry Cumberland of North Carolina is in his office. Mayfield was once married to his son, Lee, who had broken his neck and wore a brace. One night while drinking he took off the brace, tripped and killed himself. Betty was discovered trying to put the brace back on, and Cumberland, the town tyrant, had her prosecuted for murder. A local jury convicted her, but the judge set aside the verdict and declared her innocent. She left town, but Cumberland vowed to haunt her to the ends of the earth. Alessandro throws Cumberland out, hoping that rough treatment "makes him take another look at himself." This is as much theme as the novel ventures. Citing his own self-insight, Marlowe turns down Mayfield's romantic overtures.

Instead he visits Brandon, whom he accuses of pushing Mitchell over the balcony. Mitchell landed on Mayfield's balcony directly below with a broken neck. The "playback" of her ex-husband's death made her panic. Marlowe guesses that Brandon lowered the body to the ground, put it and Mitchell's luggage in his car, then dropped them at sea from a helicopter. Brandon confirms this ridiculous scenario. He is ready to pay off, but Marlowe can't be bought; he won't even shake hands with Brandon when he leaves.

Arriving back in Los Angeles, Marlowe gets two phone calls. One is from Linda Loring, who proposes marriage and asks him to come to Paris; instead Marlowe sends her a plane ticket to Los Angeles. The other call is from Umney, still seeking his information.

Title as Theme

Chandler clearly intended the title of *Playback* to indicate the circumstances of the "crime" that frightened Betty Mayfield. Finding Mitchell dead on her balcony replicates the situation in which she discovered her husband, Lee: both were drunk, both had broken necks. She was so terrified that she could not explain to Marlowe what was happening. For her the events are a replay, or "playback" in the television parlance that Chandler used.

The title has a second sense and perhaps intention. *Playback* is a "nice" novel: the principal female character is innocent and vindicated. Her enemy is sent away humiliated, by no less than the honest chief of an efficient police force. Esmeralda is a nice town, full of nice people like Joe Harms, the cabbie, and Henry Clarendon IV, the gregarious lobby-sitter. The villain victimizes rich women, for whom Chandler never before had any sympathy. In fact, the rich come off well: the town's benefactor, Miss Hellwig, has given "the hospital, a private school, a library, an art center, public tennis courts, and God knows what else" (*P*, 130). The circumstances are the reverse of what readers expected in a novel by Chandler. This makes it a "playback" in the sense that at its end, if one reexamines the earlier scenes, one

reads a different story. Seen from its conclusion, the story's rising action is innocent, rather than sinister.

The title may also have been Chandler's excuse for using the character and lines of Brigid O'Shaughnessy from Dashiell Hammett's *The
Maltese Falcon*. Chandler's novel is a "playback" in the sense that in
Betty it repeats Brigid, who leads on Sam Spade without revealing
her quest. Betty also puts Marlowe's life in jeopardy without revealing why. The clipping that Larry Mitchell waves at her is as important to the resolution as the clipping that tells Spade of the arrival of
La Paloma. But at the end Betty is revealed to be an innocent victim,
rather than a murderess; the novel "plays back" Hammett's character
in different circumstances.

Chandler's Least

Playback is clearly the least of Chandler's novels. Beyond the semi-
satiric portrait of the wealthy retirees of Esmeralda, there is little social criticism or insight. What interest the theme could offer is
unavailable until the end, when the reader learns of the death of Mayfield's ex-husband. The secondary characters are one-dimensional, and
Marlowe loses most of his code and consistency.

He now drives an expensive Oldsmobile with "pale leather seats
and the gadgets" that causes even Mayfield to comment. He stoops
to shameful impersonations without a whimper of conscience, posing
as Mayfield's ex-husband to get the room next to her and as a dope
dealer to entrap the garageman. He sleeps with his client's secretary,
though warned not to, and with Mayfield, whom he claims as his client. His trysts feature unbearably bad dialogue, such as "How can
such a hard man be so gentle?" and "Goodbye, Betty. I gave it what
I had, but it wasn't enough." His references to Linda Loring as his
true love catch readers of *The Long Goodbye* by surprise, for that relationship seemed an afterthought (*P*, 86, 155).

But *Playback* has defenders. "It still displays the characteristic
Chandlerian wit and provides certain insights into the author and his
attitude toward his work in his later years," argues Jerry Speir, citing
the thematic concept and Henry Clarendon's lecture on God: "*Playback* is no less than the last pitch from the heart of an articulate witness of a dying order and a dawning confusion." Peter Wolfe also
works hard to vindicate the novel, but admits "The book starts so

shakily that one can see why hostile critics may never have recovered from their initial letdown." Harold Orel speaks for most readers: "The means of disposing of the body is tiresomely improbable: a helicopter, and the fact that a prime suspect knows how to fly one, are mentioned for the first time [in the denouement]. The sex is gratuitous, and Marlowe turns out to be unexpectedly seedy. . . . It is dreary trash."[2]

"The Willing Captive of Romance"

Assessing Raymond Chandler's position in American letters is less perilous an undertaking than it once was. Long regarded as a "tough guy" writer, Chandler suffered from association with the detective genre most of his life. When Edmund Wilson ran down mysteries in general in the *New Yorker* in 1945, it hardly helped that he praised Chandler as the best of a bad lot.

Chandler received general recognition for his literary quality in England, where his books always sold well, before he did in the United States. By 1949 Alistair Cooke was touting him on a BBC documentary as a writer who would "be remembered when lots of what we now regard as our literary giants are buried in the school books."[3]

In the United States critics such as Bernard De Voto struggled to correct the impression left by Wilson and others that the genre, and Chandler, were subliterary. But when popular reviewers turned against the meliorated Marlowe of *The Long Goodbye* and *Playback*, it appeared that recognition of Chandler's literary excellence might be permanently sidetracked.[4]

Fortunately that did not happen. Films made from his novels kept his name before the public, and devotees of the detective novel, in and outside the academy, bolstered Chandler's reputation with dozens of articles in journals large and small. Somerset Maugham, comparing Chandler and Hammett in *The Vagrant Mood* (1945) concluded: "Chandler is the more accomplished. Sometimes Hammett's story is so complicated that you are not a trifle confused: Raymond Chandler maintains an unswerving line. His pace is swifter. He deals with a more varied assortment of persons. He has a greater sense of probability and his motivation is more plausible. Both write a nervous, colloquial English racy of the American soil. Raymond Chandler's dialogue seems to me better than Hammett's. He has an admirable aptitude for that typical product of the quick American mind, the wisecrack, and his sardonic humour has an engaging spontaneity. . . . I do not see who can succeed Raymond Chandler."[5]

Today Chandler is considered the premier American mystery writer. As Bernard Schopen wrote, "Singlehandedly, he saved the form from reimmersion in the slough of popular literature from which Hammett had raised it. . . . so effective was his commentary on the America he observed that social criticism has become a major function of the form."[6]

When *The Armchair Detective*, the Standard & Poor's of the genre, conducted a survey in 1984, readers ranked Chandler third on their list of all-time favorite authors, after Arthur Conan Doyle and Agatha Christie. The same survey revealed that Philip Marlowe trailed only Sherlock Holmes in popularity as a detective hero. Hercule Poirot and Jules Maigret, by contrast, ranked ninth and fifteenth. But the most dramatic news concerned the most popular mystery novels of all time. Of the top twenty novels, four belonged to Raymond Chandler, surpassing all other writers. *The Big Sleep* ranked third, following *The Hound of the Baskervilles* and *The Maltese Falcon*. *Farewell, My Lovely* tied for sixth, and *The Long Goodbye* for tenth. *The Lady in the Lake* placed nineteenth. Considering that Chandler wrote only seven novels, these rankings indicate a sustained level of quality unequaled by any other mystery writer.[7]

Chandler's place in mainstream American literature is more problematic. Though he produced no perfect novel, such as *The Maltese Falcon*, that would secure his place as the paradigm of an ism or school, scholars such as Philip Durham and Frank MacShane have located his inspiration and parts of his work in the realm of Theodore Dreiser, Ernest Hemingway, and T. S. Eliot. He was taken seriously by W. H. Auden, who wrote "Chandler is interested in writing, not detective stories, but serious studies of a criminal milieu, the Great Wrong Place, and his powerful but extremely depressing books should be read and judged, not as escape literature, but as works of art."[8] While it would not be true to say that Chandler's work as a body is of that caliber, it flashes quite often with verbal radiance and human passion.

It is likely that Chandler's importance will finally be realized only when the elevation of style, by writers themselves, to a position of supreme importance in twentieth-century American literature is generally recognized. As a stylist Chandler has already stood the test of fifty years, and seems likely to be just as fresh, as astonishing on the page in a hundred. Like Twain or Faulkner or Hemingway, he is a writer who advanced the technique of writing. "Chandler wrote like a slumming angel," said Ross Macdonald, "and invested the sun-blinded streets of Los Angeles with a romantic presence."[9] All subsequent writers must read him to absorb what he did.

Chandler himself would probably wish to be remembered for the ways in which he surpassed Hammett, that overpowering influence on his own work. In praise of Hammett he wrote in "The Simple Art of Murder" that his style said "things he did not know how to say, or feel the need of saying. In his hands it had no overtones, left no echo, evokes no image beyond a distant hill." In Chandler's own work language *does* all of these things. And it provides what he thought most important in writing: "a quality of redemption." Through his similes and hyperbole, Chandler summoned up a host of mythic allusions, Arthurian and American, that give his work a thematic resonance out of proportion to its structural integrity. As no other twentieth-century American writer, Chandler discovered that an enduring style is myth writ small.

Notes and References

Chapter One

    1. Frank MacShane, *The Life of Raymond Chandler* (New York: Random House, 1976), 3.
    2. *Selected Letters of Raymond Chandler*, ed. Frank MacShane (New York: Columbia University Press, 1981), 33–34; hereafter cited in text as *SL*.
    3. MacShane, *Life*, 4.
    4. Ibid.
    5. Ibid., 5.
    6. Ibid., 7–8.
    7. Ibid., 9.
    8. Ibid., 9–10.
    9. Ibid., 12.
    10. Ibid., 14.
    11. *Chandler Before Marlowe* (Columbia, S. C.: University of South Carolina Press, 1973), 3.
    12. Ibid., x.
    13. MacShane, *Life*, 16–17.
    14. *Chandler Before Marlowe*, 8–9.
    15. Ibid., xi, 67.
    16. MacShane, *Life*, 19; *Chandler Before Marlowe*, xi.
    17. *Chandler Before Marlowe*, 66–67.
    18. Ibid., 59–60.
    19. Ibid., 72, ix.
    20. MacShane, *Life*, 22–23.
    21. Ibid., 26.
    22. Chandler, "Trench Raid," #638, Box 10, Special Collections Department, Research Library, University of California, Los Angeles, hereafter cited as UCLA.
    23. MacShane, *Life*, 30.
    24. Ibid., 31.
    25. Ibid., 35–36, 39, 36.
    26. Ibid., 21–22.
    27. Ibid., 40.
    28. Ibid., 49.

Chapter Two

1. Philip Durham, "The Black Mask School," in *Tough Guy Writers of the Thirties* (Carbondale: Southern Illinois University Press, 1968), 56–57.
2. Joseph Shaw, quoted in MacShane, *Life*, 46; "Greed, Crime, and Politics," *Black Mask*, March 1931, 9.
3. *The Simple Art of Murder* (New York: Ballantine, 1972), 16; hereafter cited in text as *SAM*.
4. MacShane, *Life*, 50.
5. Ibid.
6. Edgar Allan Poe, *The Collected Works of Edgar Allan Poe*, ed. James A. Harrison, (New York: AMS Press, 1965), 14:358.
7. William Ruehlmann, *Saint with a Gun* (New York: New York University Press, 1974), 26, 28, 29.
8. Frank Gruber, *The Pulp Jungle* (Los Angeles; Sherbourne Press, 1967), 40.
9. MacShane, *Life*, 59.
10. Ibid., 63.
11. Robert M. Fogelson, *The Fragmented Metropolis: Los Angeles, 1850–1930* (Cambridge, Mass.: Harvard University Press, 1967), 218.
12. MacShane, *Life*, 73.
13. Ibid., 74.
14. Ibid., 77.
15. Ibid., 77–78.
16. Ibid., 75–76.
17. Ibid., 85.
18. Ibid., 284.
19. Ibid., 89.
20. Ibid., 96.

Chapter Three

1. MacShane, *Life*, 101.
2. Ibid., 107.
3. Ibid., 111.
4. Ibid., 110.
5. Ibid., 115.
6. Ibid., 116.
7. Ibid., 119.
8. Ibid., 123.
9. Ibid., 131.
10. Ibid., 148.
11. Ibid., 155.

12. Jon Tuska, *The Detective in Hollywood* (Garden City, N.Y.: Doubleday, 1978), 319.

13. MacShane, *Life*, 194.

14. Ibid., 197.

15. Ibid., 226.

16. Ibid., 232.

17. Ibid., 234.

18. Ibid., 245.

19. Ibid., 251.

20. Ibid., 258.

21. Ibid., 262.

22. Ibid., 265.

Chapter Four

1. Editorial, *Black Mask*, June 1936.

2. *Killer in the Rain* (New York: Ballantine, 1972), 3; hereafter cited in text as *KR*.

3. *Pick-up on Noon Street* (New York: Ballantine, 1972), 191; hereafter cited in text as *PNS*.

4. Bruce Henstell, *Sunshine and Wealth: Los Angeles in the Twenties and Thirties* (San Francisco: Chronicle Books, 1984), 53–54.

5. Ibid., 66.

6. *The Midnight Raymond Chandler* (Boston: Houghton Mifflin, 1971), 32.

7. MacShane, *Life*, 79–80.

8. Gershon Legman, *Love and Death* (New York: Breaking Point, 1949), 70.

9. "The Poodle Springs Story," Box 5, UCLA.

Chapter Five

1. Edward Margolies, *Which Way Did He Go: The Private Eye in Dashiell Hammett, Raymond Chandler, Chester Hines, and Ross Macdonald* (New York: Holmes & Meier, 1982), 44, 42.

2. Dennis Porter, *The Pursuit of Crime* (New Haven: Yale University Press, 1981), 39.

3. *The Big Sleep* (New York: Random House, 1976), 154; hereafter cited in text as *BS*.

4. See Margolies, *Which Way*, 43.

5. Legman, *Love and Death*, 69.

6. Cited in Philip Durham, *Down These Mean Streets A Man Must Go: Raymond Chandler's Knight* (Chapel Hill: University of North Carolina Press, 1963), 33–34.

7. Porter, *Pursuit of Crime*, 39, 41; Rabinowitz, Powell, and Wolfe in Peter Wolfe, *Something More Than Night: The Case of Raymond Chandler* (Bowling Green, O.: Bowling Green State University Popular Press, 1985), 117, 131.

8. Gavin Lambert, *The Dangerous Edge* (New York: Grossman, 1976), 221.

9. Durham, *Down*, 39.

10. Margolies, *Which Way*, 45.

11. Liahna K. Babener, "Raymond Chandler's City of Lies" in David Fine, ed., *Los Angeles in Fiction*. (Albuquerque: University of New Mexico Press, 1984), 126.

12. Chandler cited in Durham, *Down*, 1; Paul Skenazy, "Behind the Territory Ahead," *Los Angeles in Fiction*, 98.

13. *Farewell, My Lovely* (New York: Random House, 1976), 244; hereafter cited in text as *FML*.

14. Max Black, *Models and Metaphors: Studies in Language and Philosophy* (Ithaca, N.Y.: Cornell University Press, 1962), 40–44.

15. Cited in Durham, *Down*, 38.

16. Pendo, Durham, and Wolfe in Wolfe, *Something*, 142–43, 146; Porter, *Pursuit of Crime*, 64.

Chapter Six

1. *The High Window* (New York: Random House, 1976), 24; hereafter cited in text as *HW*.

2. See Richard Slotkin, *Regeneration Through Violence* (Middletown, Conn.: Wesleyan University Press, 1973).

3. Jacques Barzun, "The Illusion of the Real," in Miriam Gross, ed. *The World of Raymond Chandler*, (London, Weidenfeld & Nicolson, 1977), 162.

4. Ted Cohen, "Metaphor and the Cultivation of Intimacy," *On Metaphor* (Chicago: University of Chicago Press, 1978), 7–10; Keith Newlin, *Hardboiled Burlesque: Raymond Chandler's Comic Style* (Madison, Ind.: Brownstone Books, 1984), 25.

5. Wolfe, *Something*, 147.

6. MacShane, *Life*, 97, 99; Jerry Speir, *Raymond Chandler* (New York: Ungar, 1981), 45.

7. Pendo and Wolfe in Wolfe, *Something*, 158, 150, 161.

8. *The Lady in the Lake* (New York: Random House, 1976), 12, 31, 36, 62; hereafter cited in text as *LL*.

9. Dashiell Hammett, "The Scorched Face" in *The Big Knockover* (New York: Random House, 1972), 89; R. W. Lid, "Philip Marlowe Speaking," *Kenyon Review*, Spring 1969, 170.

10. Durham, *Down*, 176; Speir, *Chandler*, 57; Clive James, "The Country Behind the Hill" in Gross, ed., *World of Raymond Chandler*, 122.

11. MacShane, *Life*, 102–3.

12. Wolfe, *Something*, 175, 168.

Chapter Seven

1. *The Little Sister* (New York: Ballantine 1971), 175; hereafter cited in text as *LS*.

2. Herbert Ruhm, "Raymond Chandler: From Bloomsbury to the Jungle—and Beyond" in David Madden, ed., *Tough Guy Writers of the Thirties* (Carbondale: Southern Illinois University Press, 1968), 173; Durham, *Down*, 70.

3. Chandler to James Sandoe, 14 October 1949, UCLA.

4. MacShane, *Life*, 150–51.

5. Ruehlmann in Wolfe, *Something*, 185; Speir, *Chandler*, 63.

6. Wolfe, *Something*, 195–96; *The Long Goodbye* (New York: Ballantine, 1971), 2, 6, 37, hereafter cited in text as *LG*.

7. Natasha Spender, "His Own Long Goodbye" in Gross, ed., *World of Raymond Chandler*, 133–34.

8. MacShane, *Life*, 207; Speir, *Chandler*, 65, 77; Nolan and Palmer in Wolfe, *Something*, 195–96, 216.

Chapter Eight

1. *Playback* (New York: Ballantine, 1977), 7; hereafter cited in text as *P*.

2. Speir, *Chandler*, 78, 83; Wolfe, *Something*, 222; Harold Orel, "Raymond Chandler's Last Novel," *Central Mississippi Valley American Studies Association Journal* 2 (Spring 1961), 62.

3. "Raymond Chandler Speaking," BBC produced by Robert Pocock, transmitted 4 July 1949, UCLA.

4. Bernard De Voto, "The Easy Chair," *Harpers* 190 (1135): December 1944): 34–37.

5. Somerset Maugham, *The Vagrant Mood* (Garden City, N. Y.: Doubleday, 1952), 129.

6. Bernard Schopen, "From Puzzles to People: The Development of the American Detective Novel," *Studies in American Fiction* 7 (2):175–89.

7. "The Armchair Detective Readers' Survey," *Armchair Detective* 17 (2) (Spring 1984):128–30.

8. W. H. Auden, "The Guilty Vicarage," *Harper's Magazine* 196 (1176) (May 1948):408.

9. Ross Macdonald, introduction, *Ken Millar/Ross Macdonald: A Checklist* (Detroit: Gale Research, 1974).

Selected Bibliography

PRIMARY SOURCES

(Publication data given first American, first British, current paperbound.)

1. Novels

The Big Sleep. New York: Knopf, 1939; London: Hamilton, 1939; New York: Random House, 1976.

Farewell, My Lovely. New York: Knopf, 1940; London: Hamilton, 1940; New York: Random House, 1976.

The High Window. New York: Knopf, 1942; London: Hamilton, 1943; New York: Random House, 1976.

The Lady in the Lake. New York: Knopf, 1943; London: Hamilton, 1944; New York: Random House, 1976.

The Little Sister. Boston: Houghton Mifflin, 1949; London: Hamilton, 1949; New York: Ballantine, 1971.

The Long Goodbye. Boston: Houghton Mifflin, 1954; London: Hamilton, 1953; New York: Ballantine, 1971.

Playback. Boston: Houghton Mifflin, 1958; London: Hamilton, 1958; New York: Ballantine, 1977.

2. Principal Story Collections

Five Murderers. New York: Avon, 1944.

Five Sinister Characters. New York: Avon, 1945.

Finger Man and Other Stories. New York: Avon, 1946.

The Simple Art of Murder. Boston: Houghton Mifflin, 1950; New York: Ballantine, 1972.

Pickup on Noon Street. New York: Pocket, 1952; New York: Ballantine, 1972.

Killer in the Rain. Boston: Houghton Mifflin, 1964; London: Hamilton, 1964; New York: Ballantine, 1972.

3. Other Books

The Blue Dahlia. New York: Popular Library, 1976.

Chandler Before Marlowe: Raymond Chandler's Early Prose and Poetry. Columbia, S. C.: University of South Carolina Press, 1973.

The Notebooks of Raymond Chandler. Edited by Frank MacShane. New York: Ecco Press, 1976.

Raymond Chandler Speaking. Edited by Dorothy Gardiner and Katharine Sor-
ley Walker. Boston: Houghton Mifflin, 1977.
Selected Letters of Raymond Chandler. Edited by Frank MacShane. New York:
Columbia University Press, 1981.

4. Manuscripts
Most of Raymond Chandler's manuscripts, filmscripts, and letters are held
by the Special Collections Department of the Research Library, University of California, Los Angeles.

SECONDARY SOURCES

1. Bibliography
Bruccoli, Matthew. *Raymond Chandler: A Descriptive Bibliography*. Pitts-
burgh: University of Pittsburgh Press, 1979.
Skinner, Robert E. *The Hard-boiled Explicator*. Metuchen, N. J.: Scarecrow
Press, 1985.

2. Books
Allen, Frederick Lewis. *Only Yesterday*. New York: Harper & Row, 1931.
A cultural and political history of the twenties.
Bean, Walter. *California: An Interpretive History*. New York: McGraw-Hill,
1968.
Cawelti, John. *Adventure, Mystery, and Romance*. Chicago: University of Chi-
cago Press, 1976. A most useful book on the background of the "popu-
lar" genres.
Champigny, Robert. *What Will Have Happened*. Bloomington: Indiana
University Press, 1977. A theory of detective fiction as the purest form
of the "play" behind all literature.
Durham, Philip. *Down These Mean Streets A Man Must Go: Raymond Chan-
dler's Knight*. Chapel Hill, N. C.: University of North Carolina Press,
1963. Pioneering study of Chandler of enduring value.
Eames, Hugh. *Sleuths, Inc.* Philadelphia: J. B. Lippincott, 1978. Chapter
on Chandler examining the reality of his depiction of Los Angeles. Un-
documented and misleading.
Eisen, Jonathan, and Fine, David, eds. *Unknown California*. New York:
Macmillan, 1985. An anthology of analyses of California culture.
Fine, David, ed. *Los Angeles in Fiction*. Albuquerque: University of New
Mexico Press, 1984. Anthology of excellent pieces, including the essays
by Skenazy and Babener.

Fogelson, Robert M. *The Fragmented Metropolis: Los Angeles, 1850–1930.* Cambridge, Mass.: Harvard University Press, 1967. Scholarly study showing that Los Angeles politics was dominated by reform movements during Chandler's life.

Fox, James M. *Letters: Raymond Chandler and James M. Fox.* Santa Barbara, Calif.: Neville & Yellin, 1978. Uncollected letters between the two authors, of limited interest.

Gross, Miriam, ed. *The World of Raymond Chandler.* London: Weidenfeld & Nicolson, 1977. The most important collection of Chandler criticism, with essays by Spender, Symons, Houseman, Mason, James, and Barzun, among others.

Gruber, Frank. *The Pulp Jungle.* Los Angeles: Sherbourne Press, 1967. Fascinating portrait of hack novelists in 1920s and 1930s.

Henstell, Bruce. *Sunshine and Wealth: Los Angeles in the Twenties and Thirties.* San Francisco: Chronicle Books, 1984. Large-format picture book with excellent chapters on Prohibition and gambling ships off Santa Monica that form background of *Farewell, My Lovely.*

Lambert, Gavin. *The Dangerous Edge.* New York: Grossman, 1976. Chapter on Chandler contending his work grows from psychological shocks in early life. Limited value.

Legman, Gershon. *Love and Death.* New York: Hacker Art Books, 1963. Reprint of landmark 1949 essay on sex, sadism, murder, and misogynism in American high and low literature. Raises question of latent homosexuality in Chandler's work.

MacShane, Frank. *The Life of Raymond Chandler.* New York: Random House, 1976. The major biography of the writer. Meticulously researched, carefully and fairly written. There will be no need for any other.

McWilliams, Carey. *Southern California: An Island on the Land.* Salt Lake City: Peregrine Smith, 1983. Reprint of the classic analysis of how California culture got that way.

Madden, David, ed. *Tough Guy Writers of the Thirties.* Carbondale: Southern Illinois University Press, 1968. A seminal volume of criticism on the period, containing several excellent essays on Chandler, including Ruhm.

Margolies, Edward. *Which Way Did He Go?* New York: Holmes & Meier, 1982. Chapter on Chandler in discussion of how detective heroes and the genre respond to social values.

Newlin, Keith. *Hardboiled Burlesque: Raymond Chandler's Comic Style.* Madison, Ind.: Brownstone Books, 1984. Examination of how Chandler's handling of generic conventions, especially language, changes in the course of his development.

Nolan, William F. *The Black Mask Boys.* New York: Morrow, 1985. Superb collection of *Black Mask* stories with entertaining biographical introductions.

Pearson, Edmund. *Dime Novels.* Boston: Little, Brown, 1929. Background on antecedents of the tough guy novel, especially Old Cap Collier and Old Sleuth.

Pendo, Stephen. *Raymond Chandler on Screen: His Novels into Film.* Metuchen, N. J.: Scarecrow Press, 1976.

Porter, Dennis. *The Pursuit of Crime: Art and Ideology in Detective Fiction.* New Haven: Yale University Press, 1981. Examines the range of artistic choices within the genre and explores the underlying conservative ideology.

Ruehlmann, William. *Saint with a Gun: The Unlawful American Private Eye.* New York: New York University Press, 1974. Well-written, controversial study of historic background and morality of American detective. Chapter on Chandler.

Speir, Jerry. *Raymond Chandler.* New York: Ungar, 1981. A good general survey of Chandler's life and fiction.

Starr, Kevin. *Americans and the California Dream.* London: Oxford University Press, 1973. How the promises that sold millions of immigrants on the state in the 1920s and 1930s have been incorporated into California's daily life.

————. *Inventing the Dream: California Through the Progressive Era.* London: Oxford University Press, 1985. An examination of Southern California, Hollywood, and the rise of Socialist-Progressive politics.

Tuska, Jon. *The Detective in Hollywood.* Garden City, N.Y.: Doubleday, 1978. Hollywood's adaptations of the genre. Chapter on Chandler as a screenwriter and on movies made of his novels.

Wells, Walter. *Tycoons and Locusts: A Regional Look at Hollywood Fiction of the 1930s.* Carbondale: Southern Illinois University Press, 1973. Chapter on *Farewell, My Lovely*, showing dissolution to be the theme of L.A. regionalism.

Wolfe, Peter. *Something More Than Night: The Case of Raymond Chandler.* Bowling Green, Ohio: Bowling Green State University Popular Press, 1985. A well-researched but often grumpy study of Chandler's work, finding the author misogynic and covertly homosexual.

3. Articles

Apostolou, John L. "AKA Philip Marlowe." *Armchair Detective* 17 (1984):201–2.

Grella, George. "Murder and the Mean Streets." *Contempora* 1:1 (1970):6–15.

Guetti, James. "Aggressive Reading: Detective Fiction and Realistic Narrative." *Raritan* 2:1 (1982):133–54.

Hartman, Geoffrey. "The Mystery of Mysteries." *New York Review of Books* 18:9 (18 May 1972):31–34.

Lid, R. W. "Philip Marlowe Speaking." *Kenyon Review* 31:2 (1969):153–78.

MacDermott, K. A. "Ideology and Narrative Stereotyping: The Case of Raymond Chandler." *Clues* 2:1 (1981):77–90.

Miller, Robert Henry. "The Publication of Raymond Chandler's *The Long Goodbye.*" *Bibliographic Society of America* 63 (1969):279–90.

Rabinowitz, P. J. "Rats Behind the Wainscoting: Politics, Convention and Chandler: *The Big Sleep.*" *Texas Studies in Language and Literature* 22:2 (1980):224–45.

Schopen, Bernard. "From Puzzles to People: The Development of the American Detective Novel." *Studies in American Fiction* 7:2 (1979):175–89.

Index

Abrams, John, 16, 18
Academy, 9, 10, 147
Adams, Cleve, 31
"And Now Tomorrow," 39
Anderson, Sherwood, 96
Antigone, 128
Arbuckle, Roscoe, 30
Argosy All-Story, 26
Armchair Detective, The, 152
Atlantic, 13, 39, 41–43
Auden, W. H., 152

Babcock, Dwight, 31, 32
Babener, Liahna, 90
Ballard, W. T., 31
Balzac, Honoré de, 24
Barzun, Jacques, 8, 9, 11, 111
Baumgarten, Bernice, 44
Beadle and Adams novels, 26
Bentley, E. C., 26
Big Bear Lake, 35, 41, 67, 70
"Big Knockover, The," 22
Bishop Murder Case, The, 26
Bizet, Georges, 53
Black Mask, 19, 20, *21–24,* 27, 30,
    32–33, 52–54, 56–62, 64
Black, Max, 100–101
Bloomsbury, 8
Bogart, Humphrey, 41
Brackett, Leigh, 27, 41
Brandt, Carl, 44–45
Brasher Doubloon, The, 35

Cain, James M., 37
Carmen (character), 27, 53, 58, 68, 74,
    80, 82, 84, *86–87,* 93, 120
Carmody, Ted, *57–60,* 61–64
Carter, Nick, 26
Castle of Otranto, 24
Chamber's Journal, 7

Chandler, Cissy, 12, 14, 18–19, 27, 33,
    38–46, 54, 67, 132, 137, 147
Chandler, Florence, 1, 2, 8, 12, 14
Chandler, Raymond: adolescence, 5–7;
    becomes a writer, 19–20; birth, 1;
    Black Mask and, 19, 23–24, 32; Cali-
    fornia and, 27–30; childhood, 1–5;
    clerkship in Admiralty, 6–7; Dabney
    Oil, works for, 14–18; fired from, 18;
    England, residence in, 48–49; visits
    alone, 47; visits with Cissy, 45–46;
    death of, 50; death of Cissy, 45–46;
    Hammett, influence of, 22; Holly-
    wood, works in, 37–41; immigrates
    to United States, 11; Irish back-
    ground, 2–4, 7–8; La Jolla, lives in,
    33; London, life in, 7–11; marries
    Cissy Pascal, 14; moves frequently,
    33; Paris and Munich, lives in, 6–7;
    Public School background, 4–6; sui-
    cide threats, 46–47; World War I ser-
    vice, 12–13; wounded in, 13; writes
    The Big Sleep, 30–31; writes "The
    Blue Dahlia," 40; writes "Double In-
    demnity," 38; writes *Farewell, My
    Lovely,* 33–34; writes *The High Win-
    dow,* 35–36; writes *The Lady in the
    Lake,* 33–34; writes *The Little Sister,*
    42–43; writes *The Long Goodbye,*
    44–45; writes *Playback,* 47–49; writes
    "Strangers on a Train," 43–44

WORKS—ESSAYS:
"Genteel Artist, The," 9
"Houses to Let," 10
"Literary Fop, The," 9
"Realism and Fairyland," 9–10
"Remarkable Hero, The," 9
"Simple Art of Murder, The," 11, 39,
    153
"Tropical Romance, The," 9, 10
"Writers in Hollywood," 41

165